"The vision of Christ Commu_
and expand his kingdom amo_
ple. Having a permission-base_
conversations is essential for those who wish to faithfully embody
the mission of Jesus Christ in public spaces. Using the model described here, Christ Community Health Services has been able to
impact the lives of tens of thousands of individuals for Jesus Christ
through health care to the underserved. We are proud to pioneer
this work and now see it expand beyond our organization."

—**Shantelle Leatherwood**, CEO of Christ Community
Health Services

"Our culture is drifting further away from a Judeo-Christian
worldview. But how do you reach a drifting culture? One way is by
equipping believers to be able to engage in spiritual conversations
in ordinary and natural ways. Leveraging their experiences in a
medical environment, Jim and David help us understand the practical elements in engaging people in natural conversations with the
hope of meeting their greatest need—a relationship with Christ.
I'm grateful for this practical resource for the church as we strive
to reach a world in desperate need of Christ."

—**Ed Stetzer**, Executive Director of the Wheaton College
Billy Graham Center

"Shultz and Rogers have gathered thousands of hours of data and
research about using spiritual conversations to foster maturity of
love for Jesus and depth of Christian character. *The Practical Art of
Spiritual Conversation* is the fruit of this research and the wisdom
they have garnered from their own pilgrimages and ministries.
The book's central emphasis is unique, refreshing, and hopeful:
how to use spiritual conversations to draw people into connection
with Jesus or strengthen those connections with Jesus for believers by learning how and when to discuss key notions with people
to help them on their way. The book is a treasure-trove of deep
reflection and practical wisdom about assessing and facilitating
spiritual health and training of others to do the same. This is an
important book for our time."

—**J. P. Moreland**, Distinguished Professor of Philosophy,
Talbot School of Theology

"'Evangelism with a heart and helping hands' describes the perspective Jim Shultz and David Rogers reflect in their enjoyable book, *The Practical Art of Spiritual Conversation*. With personal examples and illustrations peppering the pages, the authors demonstrate that the gospel takes root best when the bearer of the good news understands and sympathizes with the worldview of the unevangelized person. Not since Paul Little's *How to Give Away Your Faith* (1966) has such a helpful, practical book appeared, on how to witness for Christ naturally and without fear. Any Christian desiring to share their faith will be both instructed and inspired by this book."

—**Robin Dale Hadaway**, author of *A Survey of World Missions*

"Jim Shultz and David Rogers have taken what they have learned from their years of service as spiritual advisors in healthcare settings to help Christ followers initiate important gospel conversations with unbelievers. They also offer assistance to help guide encounters with other believers in such a way as to help them take a deeper step in their walk with God. Encouraging readers to listen well and to sensitively seek opportunities for potential life-changing spiritual conversations, this wonderfully helpful and insightful book offers practical and thoughtful instruction for men and women at various stages of Christian maturity. I am delighted to recommend this highly applicable book."

—**David S. Dockery**, President of International Alliance
for Christian Education

"Here is a model for spiritual care that is respectful, appropriate in a provider/patient relationship, effective, and biblically faithful. Jim, David, and their team have refined years of experience into this practical and comprehensive guide on having meaningful spiritual conversations with patients. This is a book written, not out of theory, but out of experience over the course of hundreds of thousands of patient encounters. Every health professional who recognizes the importance of whole-person approaches to health and wants that for their patients should read this book."

—**Steve Noblett**, Executive Director of Christian Community
Health Fellowship

"*The Practical Art of Spiritual Conversation* forces me to recall and rejoice in relation to God's saving and sustaining 'conversations' with me through his listening to me (as in becoming human), walking with me, loving me—even through others. Shultz and Rogers further remind us of our call to live incarnationally and the privilege of practically 'conversing' with others as Jesus did with us—to his glory and toward helping others live in eternal 'conversation' with our Lord."

—**Frank Anderson**, Director of the Center for Racial Reconciliation at Union University

"Having meaningful spiritual conversations that can move toward a presentation of the gospel is more of an art than a technique. It is often going on a journey with a friend, not a one-time event with a stranger. It begins by loving others well and listening to others well. This book will equip you to do both."

—**Daniel L. Akin**, President of Southeastern Baptist Theological Seminary

"In *The Practical Art of Spiritual Conversation*, two highly respected Spiritual Health leaders offer practical solutions that have already impacted thousands and are destined to impact many, many more because of this book. It's a biblically-based, practical approach to how we should talk to each other in an impactful way without imposing. My hats off to Jim and David on both a job well done with their book, but more importantly, a job well lived as practitioners of practically engaging people in spiritual conversations."

—**Dan Henley**, Executive Director of the Church Developers Network

"David Rogers's father, Adrian Rogers, was my mentor and spiritual hero. In the spirit of his father, who had a tremendous heart for sharing Jesus, he and Jim Shultz have written a book much needed in our day about how to have spiritual conversations with people who need Christ. When you read it you will be blessed, but when you put its principles to work you will be an eternal blessing to others."

—**James Merritt**, host of *Touching Lives*

"If you are one of those people who love Jesus and know the call to tell others, this is for you! If you struggle with starting a conversation with friends, families, and strangers, this book is for you! Read an encouraging, simple method to let your light shine and gain the confidence to engage others about faith in Christ."

—**Hal Hoxie**, President of the Butterfield Foundation

"Shultz and Rogers vividly remind us that our life, at its core, is relational. When people know they are loved by God, and when they love God and others, joy can happen even in tough circumstances. How to get there? Conversations—real listening to understand coupled with gentle, wise questions take us deeper into relationship with God and others. This book is a gift of simple, practical relational beauty."

—**Glenn Lucke**, Founder and President of Docent Group

"The old saying 'People don't care how much you know until they know how much you care' fits this book perfectly. Jim Shultz and David Rogers have penned a powerful strategy of truth in what it means to practice the art of having spiritual conversations. When we study the life of our Lord Jesus having gospel conversations, whether it be with an immoral woman at the well, or a moral man who came to him at night, we discover Jesus was the Master of this art of connection and conversation. He knew that compassion is 'your pain in my heart,' and he listened on their terms, and he took time to let them know he understood before he responded. Jim and David teach a bigger vision of the gospel and the book will show you how to offer the Savior before you offer a solution, because in reality, the solution is the Savior. That is the gospel art of a spiritual conversation."

—**Ken Whitten**, Senior Pastor of Idlewild Baptist Church, Lutz, Florida

"I really appreciate the way Jim and David seek to encourage and equip regular Christians to engage in spiritual conversations with the people in their lives. A very helpful part of their approach is the way they spend some time on basic understandings of the gospel and discipleship. The way they go about explaining these basics of the Christian life will help every believer and will certainly help them in their spiritual conversations. I found the material and their suggestions to be very practical and understandable. They are also very encouraging and inspirational in their approach and in their call for all believers to help others move closer to Jesus."

—**David Van Kley**, Senior Pastor of Bethel Reformed Church, Sheldon, Iowa

The Practical Art of Spiritual Conversation

The Practical Art of Spiritual Conversation

Learning the *Whens* of Evangelism
and the *Hows* of Discipleship

James Harrison Shultz

AND

David Rogers

WIPF & STOCK · Eugene, Oregon

THE PRACTICAL ART OF SPIRITUAL CONVERSATION
Learning the *Whens* of Evangelism and the *Hows* of Discipleship

Wipf & Stock
An Imprint of Wipf and Stock Publishers
199 W. 8th Ave., Suite 3
Eugene, OR 97401

www.wipfandstock.com

PAPERBACK ISBN: 978-1-7252-9481-3
HARDCOVER ISBN: 978-1-7252-9482-0
EBOOK ISBN: 978-1-7252-9483-7

03/30/21

Contents

Acknowledgments

A BOOK ON SPIRITUAL conversations is worthless if not tried through real life encounters with real people. This work comes from tens of thousands of conversations performed by the Spiritual Health team at Christ Community Health Services in Memphis, Tennessee: Pastor Dirk Martre, Dr. David Rogers, Minister Grace Hilton-Young, Dr. Edwin Alston, Mr. Johnny Doe, and Pastor Robert Brumsey. Their commitment to loving people by leading them closer to Jesus through spiritual conversations is relentless, and I am proud to be on their team! Additionally, thank you to Rev. Dr. Jackie Gatliff and Mrs. Jill Hollingsworth, who served our team in years past and helped contribute to this work.

Two organizations have contributed significantly to this work. First, the Butterfield Foundation (and specifically Dierdre McCool) has encouraged, supported, and provided a broad opportunity to share this information beyond Memphis. Without their support, this would not have come to fruition. Second, Christ Community Health Services has allowed us to pioneer the work of this framework through our primary care clinics and has offered unwavering support all along the way. Specifically, I want to thank Christ Community Health Services' CEO, Mrs. Shantelle Leatherwood, for her commitment to my team and to the gospel of Jesus Christ. Because of CCHS and Shantelle, this is not just "theory," but is lived out every day with real people.

Thank you to Dr. Corey Latta, who has shepherded us through the whole writing process. From proposal, to bringing clarity, to editing, Dr. Latta has given so much to this work and could have easily been named as another author. I am thankful for his mentoring in writing.

I want to thank my wife, Dr. Laura Shultz. Her love supports me through everything. And seeing how hard she works at her profession, at being an incredible mom, and at being an excellent wife inspires me to be a better man. She is the love of my life, and without her support I am not sure I could do much of anything. She embodies Prov 31:29, which says, "Many women do noble things, but you surpass them all." And thank you to my boys, Samuel, Jeremiah, and Isaiah, who are our joy.

Finally, I thank the Lord. By help of the Holy Spirit I truly believe the Lord has gifted us with this book that we might help further the Kingdom of Jesus Christ for his glory. As we release it into the world, we entrust God to do his work. Our heart and desire has been simply to "equip the saints for the work of ministry, for building up the body of Christ" (Eph 4:12).

Jim Shultz, DMin

AFTER YEARS OF EXPERIENCE with a wide array of Christian ministries in various contexts around the world, I've had the joy and privilege of serving most recently as Spiritual Health Advisor at Christ Community Health Services in Memphis, Tennessee. I'm immensely grateful for the opportunity to partner together with Dr. Jim Shultz and the rest of the staff at CCHS as we seek to minister the love of Christ through high-quality healthcare to the underserved, and more specifically as Spiritual Health Advisors through life-giving spiritual conversations with the wide variety of patients who visit us day after day at the clinics. These years with CCHS have provided me with both a fascinating ministry workshop and a strategic missionary platform as I've had the privilege to engage in many hours of fruitful dialogue with the hundreds of patients the Lord has brought my way during this time.

My greatest supporter through it all has been my lovely wife and life partner, Kelly, who has faithfully stood by my side throughout a winding journey of adventures, victories, and trials, as we climb the hill of life together. I'm also blessed beyond measure by my two outstanding sons, Jonathan and Stephen, and my wonderful daughter-in-law, Shelby.

Most of all, I thank my matchless Lord and Savior Jesus, who has beckoned me to walk side by side with him and bear his yoke together with him through all these years as he teaches me what it means to be gentle and lowly in heart.

Soli Deo Gloria.

David Rogers, PhD

Introduction

THE GOAL OF THIS book is simple: to equip Christians in the practical art of spiritual conversation so that they can meaningfully and substantially encourage each person to take one step in their life toward Christ. At Christ Community Health Services in Memphis, Tennessee, we use the very framework presented in this book to have spiritual conversations with patients in a primary care setting. As a result, our little team of six people had 12,867 spiritual conversations in 2019. We shared the gospel of salvation 1,320 times. We referred 845 people to local churches. We saw seventy-nine people recommit their lives to Christ and seventy-five accept Christ as Savior. Of course, there is much more life change that took place that cannot be captured by statistics: Tears wept as one feels the release of an emotional or spiritual burden they had been feeling. A change from fear and anxiety to peace and trust in God through the simple act of prayer. A person who began the conversation disconnected from God gently reminded of God's great love and grace. We take no credit for these things. We believe this is God's work. And as we faithfully seek to engage others in spiritual conversations, he will do his work of changing lives.

Consider one patient who I will call Steve. Steve was a young man and was transitioning back to society after being jailed. He did not yet have a place to stay and was nervous about re-entering "normal life" after prison. As he talked with one of our team members, he said he had no concept of God or Jesus. He seemed receptive to a conversation, though. Following God's lead and the framework shared here, our teammate shared with Steve about Jesus and how God held his life in his hands. As he heard the message of the gospel, he began to weep. He asked, "Would Jesus really do this for me?" Yes, he would. And that day Steve began a relationship with Jesus Christ. Eventually, he received a Bible and help on reading it. He learned to pray. He even received information on churches that would walk with him through re-entry. God changed Steve's life through a spiritual conversation and continued to change his life with each conversation since. All our teammate did was follow God's lead while following the framework you'll learn in this book.

Every Christian should be prepared to talk about Jesus with anyone (1 Pet 3:15; Matt 28:19). This is not just about *evangelism* nor is it just about *discipleship*. This is about helping any willing person move closer to Christ, regardless of whether they are a staunch atheist or a seasoned believer. This requires a reorientation of foundational Christian buzzwords such as *evangelism*, *discipleship*, and *gospel*. And we need wisdom for when to employ each. That wisdom for the *whens* and *hows* of evangelism and discipleship is the essence of spiritual conversation and exactly what this book hopes to provide.

There are many who are eager to evangelize and daily share the good news of a saving relationship with Jesus. We write to this person so that they may know when it may be inappropriate or even harmful to share this good news. We write to this person so they may be equipped to have meaningful conversations with not just the lost but also with the hurting and the found.

There are many who love Jesus and walk with him but never seem to get around to having spiritual conversations with anyone. We write to them so that they may know how they might lovingly and thoughtfully engage a person spiritually and in doing so will share the gospel more and help others progress in their love for Jesus.

There are many who feel stuck in their discipleship efforts. They do everything they know to grow in their faith, but in their communication with God they feel like a caller who keeps getting sent to voicemail. We write to this person so that they may have a bigger vision of what it means to have a relationship with Christ, and in doing so help fellow sojourners when they feel stuck.

There are many who see no connection between the gospel as they've received it and the many important things they do each day. Their walk with God doesn't integrate with the many important things they do each day, such as working, parenting, playing, or eating. We write to them so that they may know that God cares deeply about even seemingly mundane activities and can truly integrate their faith into everything they do.

The general framework is simple enough. In our spiritual conversations we need to first seek to *understand* and then *respond*. We will get to this in chapter 3, and it will take nuancing to be useful. But before we can get there, we need to understand the gospel and what it means to be spiritually healthy.

Jim and David

1

Spiritual Health

Understanding Spiritual Health

IMAGINE GOING TO THE doctor with an ache or pain in your leg that hurts so badly you can barely walk. Your purpose for being there in that exam room describing your ailment is simple: You believe that this person has the knowledge to help you get back to health. This scenario carries some assumptions. It assumes that this is your doctor and not your mechanic. It assumes that you and the doctor agree on some definition of health. It assumes that this doctor knows medical interventions that will help you get to this shared idea of health. Further, it assumes that the person you're talking to actually has the training and knowledge to diagnose what's ailing you so that you can apply the right therapy. Without these assumptions, the scenario is senseless.

Now, as Christians, God calls us to be like physicians. Our task goes well beyond a hurting leg. God invites us to facilitate health holistically—not just for ourselves, but in all of creation. This, too, assumes many things. It assumes we're Christians and actually follow the restorative ways of Christ. It assumes that we agree with God on what health looks like in this world. It assumes that we've taken the time to learn how to diagnose what's wrong in creation. It assumes that we have access to interventions that might help facilitate health. Without these assumptions, true change remains impossible.

How do we get to the place where we can excel at our task as God's physicians? Before we can discuss how healing works, we must begin with a shared idea of what health is.

Shared Idea of Health

In order to be spiritual physicians, we need to have a clear idea of what it means to be spiritually healthy. We can't possibly diagnose what's wrong if we don't know what's right. It would do no good to speak of someone being healed from an illness if we had no understanding of health. Categories such as illness assume there's a way it should be. If that weren't the case, everything would be a series of arbitrary experiences that are neither healthy nor unhealthy. How would we even begin to describe what holistic health would look like?

Biblically, the word that's used to describe reality in total, perfect health is the Hebrew word *shalom*. Cornelius Plantinga defines it this way:

> The webbing together of God, humans, and all creation in justice, fulfillment, and delight is what the Hebrew prophets call shalom. We call it peace, but it means far more than mere peace of mind or a cease-fire between enemies. In the Bible, shalom means universal flourishing, wholeness and delight—a rich state of affairs in which natural needs are satisfied and natural gifts fruitfully employed, a state of affairs that inspires joyful wonder as its Creator and Savior opens doors and welcomes the creatures in whom he delights. Shalom, in other words, is the way things ought to be.[1]

Shalom is God's picture for health. This isn't just spiritual health as we usually understand it, but the health of all things. This vision for health includes everything, because in God's design everything is spiritual. Because everything is spiritual, spiritual health means health in all areas. So as Christians, we partner

---

1. Plantinga, *Not the Way It's Supposed to Be*, 10.

with God in his great work of restoring health—*shalom*—to every aspect of all reality.

This *shalom* vision of health includes moments like when a crossing guard helps a child cross the street safely, when you cook your family dinner, or when a doctor sets your broken leg. It includes prayer, Bible study, and fasting. It includes small group Bible study or coffee with a friend. It includes doing your job well or loving your family. It includes overseas missions and local soup kitchens. It involves government, social media, trimming trees, and advances in technology. Everything is spiritual.

This may be new to you. Many of us have been given a vision for spiritual health that is only about saving souls. As a result, understanding spiritual health in such broad terms under the banner of *shalom*—the health of all things—is hard for us to reconcile. But if God really is inviting us to be his physicians restoring health in the world, and that invitation assumes we agree on what health is, we need to get this right. We need a vision for health that aligns with God's understanding of health.

Jesus casts a vision for what *shalom* looks like when he speaks of the kingdom of God. Jesus spoke of the kingdom more than anything else because the definition of health was crucial to his mission. And it always has been. When the prophet Jeremiah charged the false teachers of his time, it was because they claimed they'd brought about healing, when in reality their understanding of health fell short. As Jer 8:11 says, "They have healed the wound of my people lightly, saying, 'Peace [shalom], peace [shalom],' when there is no peace [shalom]." Jeremiah was confronting those whose vision for *shalom* was too small. A superficial healing won't do. We're not compartmentalized people who have a spiritual part of us that's separate from everything else.

How might we be tempted to have too small of a vision for *shalom*? Humans have many aspects: physical, relational, social, intellectual, and emotional. When Christians try to focus only on the spiritual part of someone's humanity with no regard for the rest, it's superficial, because it ignores humans as God created them. It would be like reading chapters 23 to 25 of a fifty-chapter novel and assuming you know the whole story. You don't. You couldn't. You're missing critical portions of the beginning, character development, plotline, climax, and resolution. When we treat people as if only their spiritual lives matter, we miss key parts of how God made people, and as a result we provide superficial healing.

Let's go back to the physician's office. We may not think of the healing of our leg as something spiritual. After all, it's our physical body that's in need of mending. But this compartmentalizing doesn't seem to match the New Testament story. Matthew 4:23 and 9:35 offer summary statements of Jesus' ministry and tell us clearly that he didn't just preach and teach, but healed diseases as well. When Jesus described neighbor love (Luke 10:25–37), he included things like bandaging wounds (10:34), giving a ride to the hospital (10:34), and covering someone's bills (10:35). And this more holistic vision of restoration isn't just about physical healing. When Jesus says that ministry to "the least of these" (Matt 25:31–46) is counted as being done for him, he had in mind giving people food or water (25:35), clothing those who are naked (25:36), welcoming strangers, and even visiting the imprisoned (25:36). Healing and restoration in any area is spiritual healing.

In order to restore *shalom* in our lives and in the lives of others, it requires us to fix any broken thing we find, even if we wouldn't normally categorize it as spiritual. God invites us as his followers to partner with him in restoring *shalom*. This seems like an impossible task, because this world is so tragically broken. After all, the world isn't in a state of *shalom*. What happened? What went wrong?

What Has Gone Wrong?

God created this world as good and intended for it to exist in *shalom*, or perfect, holistic health. This perfect, holistic health is spiritual health. Not only does this mean that we should live in a perfect relationship with God, but also in relationship with others, and that every aspect of our world should lead to flourishing for all people as well as all of creation. Just a few minutes looking at news headlines, however, makes clear that this isn't the world we live in.

What's gone wrong? Sin.

Wait. Are we really saying that all the brokenness we experience in this world is because of sin? Does that mean that sin is the reason for awful things like childhood cancer? What sin did they commit to deserve that? Is sin why tsunamis happen? Are nations with less natural disasters less sinful than nations with more tornados?

Most of us are uncomfortable blaming the specific brokenness we experience on sin—and for good reason. A child doesn't sin, then get cancer. A nation struck with natural disaster is not necessarily more sinful than one that's free of disaster. After all, God "makes his sun rise on the evil and on the good, and sends rain on the just and on the unjust" (Matt 5:45). The reason we're uncomfortable attributing the brokenness we experience in the world to sin is because we don't view sin broadly enough. We need to distinguish between *sins, sin,* and *Sin.*

- *sins*: Many would define *sins* as our individual mistakes or violations of God's laws. And that's true. When we break one of the Ten Commandments, for example, it's sin. But sin is even bigger than our individual violations of God's law.

- *sin*: We all know that we can do the right thing for the wrong reasons. And when we do, it's sin. Jesus confronted the Pharisees about this very thing, saying that they drew near to God with their lips, but their hearts were far from him (Matt 15:7–9, quoting Isa 29:13). While they weren't necessarily committing *sins* (although in many cases they actually were), they were still sinful in their hearts. Much of the thrust of Jesus' "you've heard it said" statements (Matt 5:20–48) are to point out this heart aspect of sin. So, we can avoid mistakes or even direct violations of God's laws and still sin. But *sin* is even bigger than that!

- *Sin*: We call this one "capital-S sin." This is the brokenness present in this world warping and decaying every good thing

God created. Sin's ripple effect touches everything in the whole world. This exists regardless of our *sins* (individual mistakes) or our *sin* (wicked hearts). Cancer strikes not because someone sinned or made an individual mistake, but because *Sin* is in the world. Tsunamis wipe out a city, not necessarily because the people are sinful or have hearts far from God, but because *Sin* has marred God's good earth. *Sin* refers to the brokenness we all experience regardless of our mistakes or even our hearts.

The good news, the gospel, is that Jesus Christ came to fix it all: *sins*, *sin*, and *Sin*. Jesus came to restore *shalom*.

As physicians we are called to diagnose the illness and offer a cure. What will restore shalom? The gospel!

In the same way we may be uncomfortable talking about sin because our definition is too small, most of us have too small of a definition of the gospel. For many of us, the word *gospel* means something like this: *Jesus Christ died and rose again so that I can go to heaven when I die.*

But here's a very dangerous question: *What might be the problem with that definition of the gospel?*

Isn't it true that Jesus died and rose again? And doesn't that truth mean I get to go to heaven when I die? What could be the problem? Well, first of all, it's somewhat irrelevant to my life right now. It's about what happens when I die. Other than a little bit of peace or assurance, it doesn't necessarily change anything in my life or the world around me. Second, it doesn't fix any of the things I really care about. It doesn't change cancer or racism or tsunamis or hunger or corruption or evil. It just offers me a promise of escape from those things when I die. But nothing implicit in that statement of the gospel has power to fix them. If we really think about it, that definition of the gospel is selfish. That's the gospel applied only to me.

What's wrong with the definition of the gospel that says, *Jesus Christ died and rose again so that I can go to heaven when I die?* Well, nothing, in one sense. This statement is absolutely true. Jesus Christ did die and rise again. And because that's true, you get to go to heaven when you die. But in the same way that our view of sin is too small, our view of our Savior and his gospel is too small. Because sin is bigger than we think, the gospel of Jesus must be much bigger as well. Jesus' death and resurrection means all broken things will be restored: *sins, sin* and *Sin*. Everything in all creation will be restored to God and his ways. *Shalom* will come because of, through, and by Jesus. The gospel is true, and that means you and I will one day live in this perfect world of *shalom* that God intended for us.

This expands our view of the gospel beyond just me when I die to include the restoration of everything. Jesus came to save me, but he also came to restore everything that's broken. He doesn't just come to rescue us out of it, but to redeem all things back to *shalom*. So, what do we mean by *gospel*? *The gospel is God's activity of restoring and redeeming all things in all of the universe to relationship with him and back to his design.*

Think of the way Jesus talks about his mission and his gospel. In Luke 4:18–19, Jesus gives the thesis statement for his messiahship:

> *The Spirit of the Lord is upon me, because he has anointed me to proclaim good news to the poor. He has sent me to proclaim liberty to the captives and recovering of sight to the blind, to set at liberty those who are oppressed, to proclaim the year of the Lord's favor.*

This verse is almost entirely about fixing broken things. And not just things we consider spiritual, but poverty, imprisonment, illness, and oppression. This is a holistic vision of the gospel that restores true *shalom*. Fast-forward to the book of Revelation where God casts a vision for heaven and ultimate restoration. We don't see an escape from this broken world. Instead, we see the perfect world of the Garden of Eden from Genesis restored as God returns to dwell again with humans and redeem what he intended in the beginning. Revelation 21:3–5 says,

> *And I heard a loud voice from the throne saying, "Behold, the dwelling place of God is with man. He will dwell with*

them, and they will be his people, and God himself will
be with them as their God. He will wipe away every tear
from their eyes, and death shall be no more, neither shall
there be mourning, nor crying, nor pain anymore, for the
former things have passed away." And he who was seated
on the throne said, "Behold, I am making all things new."
Also, he said, "Write this down, for these words are trust-
worthy and true."

God initiated through Jesus' death and resurrection the restoration of all things back to what he intended. We see this throughout Scripture, specifically revealed with Christ in his first coming,
and ultimately completed when Christ returns. God is actively
fixing broken things, but he doesn't stop there. He wants all things
to flourish as designed. This means that forgiveness of sins is not
an end, but a beginning toward life in connection with God; we as
humans were designed to live abundantly in relationship with the
living God in this world he's given to us.

Why is this bigger vision of the gospel important? Because
we need to make sure that we agree with God and his Word on
what spiritual health is. And the gospel gives us a glimpse of how
we can be restored back to that health and how we can participate with God as his practitioners of *shalom*. As it relates to our
spiritual conversations, we can have confidence that even the most
mundane aspects of life are avenues to a spiritual conversation.
The gospel changes not just our spiritual lives when we die, but
every aspect of all of creation now. As physicians called by God we
must diagnose where people are living out of line with God and his
ways and offer God's cure for people infected with sin.

2

Diagnosing the Illness

IF THE GOSPEL IS God's activity of restoring all things in all of the universe to relationship with him and back to his design, then as physicians called by God, we must diagnose where people are living out of line with God and his ways and offer God's cure for people infected with sin, as we all are.

If this is our task in the art of spiritual conversation, what spiritual illnesses might be prevalent?

Illness One: Christians Who Don't Follow Christ

"I'm a Christian," he said. I (Jim) asked some questions to find out where this man was spiritually, and those words slipped off his tongue as if he'd said them a thousand times. There was an assurance and conviction behind his words that made me a believer, too—that is, until he kept talking. Upon exploring exactly how he used the term *Christian*, it became clear that there was a mismatch between what it means to be a Christian in reality and what he meant by the word *Christian*. He wasn't trying to be dishonest. He believed his words. But he didn't fully understand what it meant to be a follower of Christ.

I live in the South, specifically in the Bible Belt. Nearly everyone I know says that they're a Christian, when asked. Further, upon meeting someone for the first time, it's not uncommon to be asked, "Where do you go to church?" Yet, for all the religiosity in the South, I often notice a gap between what it means to be a Christian and how people live out their actual faith in Christ. This may be stating the obvious, but calling yourself a Christian doesn't mean a lot these days.

The first illness: *When someone says they are a Christian, it does not always match what it actually means to follow Christ.*

Illness Two: Unhealthy Individualism

"A squirrel dying in front of your house may be more relevant to your interests right now than people dying in Africa." Mark Zuckerberg, the founder and CEO of Facebook, used those words to explain that a person's individual interest is the standard for how the social media site determines your newsfeed. The assumption is that you're more interested in news that is oriented to you personally than to anything or anyone else.

A cultural study by social psychologist Geert Hofstede indicated that among the highest and most deeply held values of Americans, individualism is the most highly regarded of all.[1] There are many characteristics that led to this high rating. In an individualistic culture, most people:

- focus primarily on taking care of themselves and their immediate family

- have a self-oriented interpretation of the world that constantly asks, "How does this affect me?"

- find the basis for their identity in individual terms rather than group or collective terms

- expect and protect the right to a private life

- emphasize personal achievement and initiative over group/organizational achievement

1. Hofstede, "National Cultures in Four Dimensions," 46–74.

I would imagine that if you talked to most Christians, they'd say that individualism in matters of faith is a good thing. In America, we express this value of individualism in the way we express our faith. Christian individuals, and even most churches, tend to focus on one's own personal belief in God above all else. Churches focus on *your* response to the message rather than *our* response to Christ. Countless studies have shown that many young adults are drifting from and abandoning the church but at the same time maintain that they have a personal relationship with Jesus. To complicate matters further, it's considered taboo to discuss religion in social situations. In general, most Americans would prefer to relegate matters of faith to one's private life, where others have no authority.

While we don't wish to de-emphasize the need for an individual approach to faith in Christ, we refuse to accept the idea that faith is merely an individual, private affair. Jesus' death has implications for our individualism. An individual "faith" doesn't take into account one's relationship with other Christians. But it must. There's no way to approach the Christian faith as merely an individual; our faith always requires relating to and loving God and neighbor. You can't be a Christian without love, and you can't love without another person to love. Second Corinthians 5:14–15 says,

> For the love of Christ controls us, because we have concluded this: that one has died for all, and therefore all have died; and he died for all, that those who live might no longer live for themselves but for him who for their sake died and was raised.

When we live, we don't live unto ourselves. Following Christ mandates that we live unto him in all areas of our life. And to live unto him means we must love him and others as well as live for him and others.

The second illness: *When we approach our Christian faith through the lens of individualism, we lose much of what it means to be a Christian.*

Illness Three: Small Gospel Approach to Life

Remember in chapter 1 when we said we needed a bigger vision for the gospel? Just like diabetes and coronary artery disease are two separate diagnoses that often exist at the same time in the same person, unhealthy individualism is often a comorbid illness that perpetuates a small gospel approach to life. It's a *me-sized* faith that's understood only in terms of a small gospel. Once my faith is shrunk down to me, it becomes privatized. My faith will be confined to the world of my inner experience only and eventually will become irrelevant to the rest of life. Once this occurs, this type of faith can never rise to the level of the gospel of the kingdom that Jesus described in terms of *shalom*.

This is why we need the bigger vision of the gospel that was introduced in chapter 1. The gospel is certainly about me and my life (and when I die), but it's about so much more than that. If we miss the bigger gospel, we might miss the most important aspects of the Christian faith. One way to describe two different ways of approaching the gospel is the "small gospel" approach and the "big gospel" approach.[2]

The question of the small gospel is this: *If you were to die tonight, why should God let you into heaven?* Why is this a small gospel question? It's small because the question casts faith purely in terms of my own personal salvation and neglects God's bigger redemptive plan. God is not just redeeming me personally but redeeming all of creation to his lordship. This question focuses our attention on life after death and fails to show the relevance of life here and now.

It's not necessarily a bad question. In fact, we've asked this very question to hundreds of people in hopes of having an opportunity to share the gospel. It's a useful question. If, however, the whole of our faith is about what happens when we die, we will struggle to see how or why our lives should change now. Life-change is neither expected nor does it naturally flow from the answer to that

2. Willard, "Gospel of the Kingdom."

small-gospel question. The question is only concerned with securing a place after death, not living a life with Christ now.

The question of the big gospel is this: *If you do not die tonight, how will your life be different tomorrow because of a relationship with Jesus?* This question places the focus on how Christ's gospel impacts me now. It lifts my eyes from my own personal salvation and calls me to consider how my life fits into the much bigger redemptive story God is unfolding in this world. If the gospel doesn't impact every aspect of my life and all of reality, isn't it too small of a gospel? The gospel is nothing if it's not life-changing, let alone world-changing.

The third illness: *A small gospel approach to life leads to a selfish life.*

Diagnosis

These three illnesses are intimately related. While not an exhaustive list of the problems we face, they do give you a glimpse of some of the challenges in approaching spiritual conversations. In our Western context, when people misunderstand what it means to be a Christian (illness one), it's usually because they have an unhealthy attachment to individualism (illness two), which will result in a smaller gospel approach to following Christ (illness three). The root problem is individualism, because individualism keeps the focus on me rather than Christ. Individualism is an illness like malnourishment. It's not that someone is dead, but they are grossly deprived of what they need to be healthy. The disease of individualism needs to be diagnosed and treated. If we were diagnosing someone for an individualistic faith, here are some symptoms we would look for.

Symptoms of an Individualistic Christian

- *Church is not a priority.* "If I go to church at all, I don't have people who know me beyond a superficial level."

- *Discipleship isn't a priority and is haphazard.* "It feels like exercise. I know it's important, but I struggle to have a clear plan that I follow through on doing."

- *Connection with God is through isolated, non-relational means.* "My primary plan for spiritual growth involves something that doesn't require relationships or community—a podcast, author, or worship song."

- *Personal conviction trumps all.* "What I think or feel ultimately influences my decisions. My perspective negates any other information or perspectives."

- *Faith isn't integrated with the rest of life.* "I can't articulate a meaningful connection between Jesus and things like my money, my career, or my physical health."

- *Faith is expressed in only private terms.* "I might share my own belief about faith issues, but I wouldn't say that it's necessarily true for everyone. I'm hesitant to persuade people of other faiths to believe in Christ, because I shouldn't impose my beliefs on others."

Even if these symptoms don't describe you, no doubt you get the sense that these are common ways in which others approach faith. While having an individual or personal relationship with Christ is foundational and important, the *ism* of individualism transforms a good thing into an idol. Individualism shrinks our faith and makes God in my image—at worst—or puts my faith almost entirely in my control—at best.

Many of us can fall into this same trap in our spiritual conversations. We'll try to help someone grow in Christ, but do so in merely private, individualistic ways. We'll only suggest more prayer or more emphasis on our "quiet time" Bible study. And these things are foundationally important. But what happens when more prayer and personal Bible study leave us stagnant? Perhaps there's more that God is doing to cause us to grow in him.

Though these illnesses lead us to being unhealthy, anemic, and woefully short of all God has for us, God doesn't require us to think and believe in all the right ways in order to enter into a loving relationship with him. He'll patiently call us to a greater vision for what he's doing in this world. As those called to help diagnose and treat spiritual health, we must not lose sight of this bigger vision of what it means to be a Christian. When we have spiritual conversations, we'll not stop at helping someone to "become a Christian," but go on to help them practice a bigger gospel life. This doesn't stop with their personal "quiet time," but impacts every aspect of their (and our) world. We partner with God in his work to restore *shalom*, the full expression of a relationship with God and his ways.

What should it mean when we say we're Christians, in light of this bigger gospel? To use Christianese: I don't simply "accept Jesus into my heart" so I can go to heaven when I die. It does mean that. But it means much more than that. Instead, we need to recognize that Jesus is the gracious, loving, and sovereign ruler of *all*. The big, true, God-sized gospel is one where Jesus reigns over the entire universe, not just "my heart." When I say that I'm a Christian, it must not be like a hobby ("I'm a gardener") or even a profession ("I'm a chef"); being a Christian means every aspect of life and everything in all of creation is ruled by King Jesus. And until I get there, God has sanctifying work to do. Thankfully, he has promised to continue and complete it (Phil 1:6).

When we approach spiritual conversations, we can't lose sight of this greater, bigger-gospel vision for what it means to be a Christian. This will change what we consider to be the goal of a spiritual conversation.

Treatment

Let's return to the doctor's office from chapter 1. She has successfully diagnosed the problem: You have a broken leg. Imagine she sends you home upon diagnosis. That would be frustrating, because what you really need is to be restored to health. The goal isn't just diagnosis. Diagnosis isn't enough.

Let's say the doctor resets the broken bone in your leg, putting your leg in a cast, and maybe even gives you something for the pain. Technically, you're healed, aren't you? Well, yes and no. The bone is put back right, but there's a much longer process involved to be healthy again. You need more than a one-time fix. You need healing. Let's say a few months later the bone is healed and the cast comes off, and the doctor sees no need for physical therapy. Why would she? The bone's healed! The problem, though, is that one of your legs is still significantly weaker than the other. While one part of your leg's healed, other parts still need care. She says, "You came to me with a broken bone: the bone isn't broken any longer." This would be a problem, wouldn't it? The ultimate goal is not a healed bone, but a fully functioning leg.

As Christians, the goal isn't just to be saved—as foundationally important as that is—but to live all of life fully in relationship with the Lord Jesus Christ and according to his ways. The Christian life begins with a saving relationship with Jesus but can't end there. What we're presenting here is a different way of thinking about our spiritual health, which will have implications for our spiritual conversations.

What lies ahead is a framework for spiritual conversations rooted in a bigger gospel understanding of the Christian life based on tens of thousands of spiritual conversations, complemented by practical tools for how to apply this to your own life. If you're like the healthcare students we train, you want to just get to the practical stuff. That's certainly understandable. But, like most things, it's critical that we understand the *why* before we get to the *how*. You can't bypass this part and be an excellent practitioner. This process will give us eyes to see and wisdom for the *whens* and *hows*.

3

A Framework for Spiritual Conversations

As WE MENTIONED IN the last chapter, we'll now introduce the initial framework for spiritual conversations based on a bigger gospel understanding of the Christian life. The goal of this framework is to equip Christians in the practical art of spiritual conversation so that they can meaningfully and substantially encourage each person toward growth in Christ.

Before you can help someone else, the gospel needs to have an effect on your own life. Life in Christ isn't simply something to be passed on to others. God changes you first, then he leads you to give life in him away. So, let's start with you. Think through how this impacts *you* before considering how to help *someone else*. Let God speak to your heart about how you can live more fully under the lordship of King Jesus. As you do, you'll more humbly and organically engage in meaningful spiritual conversations with others about their faith. We'll get to the very practical side of this in later chapters. For now, take an honest assessment of your own life and consider how you can fall more deeply in love with Christ and live more fully in his gospel.

We've offered a definition of the gospel, which is this: *The Gospel is God's activity of restoring all things in all of the universe back to relationship with him and back to his design.*

This is broader than what most of us mean when we say the world *gospel* and therefore requires a framework by which we reorient to the Christian life. What does it mean to live in relationship with God and according to his design? All of God's ways and expectations for us boil down to two simple things. When asked about the greatest commandment, Jesus went beyond the question to offer a simple summary of all the expectations God has for us.

> *And he said to him, "You shall love the Lord your God with all your heart and with all your soul and with all your mind. This is the great and first commandment. And a second is like it: You shall love your neighbor as yourself. On these two commandments depend all the Law and the Prophets"* (Matt 22:37–40).

This is the vision for the bigger gospel life. This is what it means to live in relationship with God and according to his design. A fully healthy spiritual life is one where we love God with all that we are and then in turn love our neighbors as we would love ourselves. Everything God desires for your life depends on love relationships. These love relationships are the goal. Jesus, in his final prayer, says, "you [the Father] have given him [Jesus] authority over all flesh, to give eternal life to all whom you have given him. And this is eternal life, that they know you the only true God, and Jesus Christ whom you have sent" (John 17:2–3).

If we want to live in a love relationship with God, we need to be with him where he is. That's what happens in a relationship, isn't it? We have to be present with that person. Jesus has come to us and made himself accessible to us. If we desire a relationship with him, we need to choose to be with him where he is.

We want to suggest to you that God reveals in Scripture four places where you can reliably find him. This means you must choose to be with him in those places if you want to be near to him. Each of these four places is intimately related to what Jesus said are the greatest commandments: to love God and love others. Spiritual health and therefore spiritual growth will always have to do with cultivating your love for God and love for others.

A Vision for the Bigger Gospel Life

- Love God
- Love Others

Each of these aspects of spiritual growth has an inward and an outward expression. Inwardly, there's a way our identity is formed by love for God and love for others. That same love is expressed outwardly as we choose to live in ways that are consistent with who we are in Christ. What are these inward and outward expressions of our love?

- Love God
  - Inward: *spirit*
  - Outward: *way, truth, life*
- Love Others
  - Inward: *community of faith*
  - Outward: *mission*

We'll very briefly introduce these concepts here but go deeper later.

Spirit: the inward aspect of loving God

If we want to love, or connect with Jesus inwardly, we connect with him in our *spirit*. In John 4:24, Jesus says that anyone who wants to worship God must worship him in spirit and in truth. Our spirit is the part of us that loves God at a personal, individual level. We give and receive love from God inwardly in our spirit.

Community of Faith: the inward aspect of loving others

Loving *others* inwardly is about how we connect with a *community of faith* or church. This isn't just about the people, though. This is also a way we connect with Jesus himself. Think about what Jesus said in Matt 18:20: "For where two or three are gathered in my name, there am I among them." Jesus ties his presence to those gathering in his name. If the Body of Christ is his church, then we must love those within that body.

Way, Truth, Life: the outward aspect of loving God

God calls us outside of ourselves to express our love for him outwardly. We show our outward love of God by living according to his *ways, truth,* and *life* (John 14:6). As we live according to God's ways, God's truth, and life as God designed it, there's a sense in which we connect with him. First John 5:3 says, "For this is the love of God, that we keep his commandments. And his commandments are not burdensome." We must obey his ways as a means of loving him.

Mission: the outward aspect of loving others

God calls us beyond ourselves and the community of faith out into his *mission.* Jesus ties his presence to the Great Commission of Matt 28:19–20, where he said, "Go therefore and make disciples of all nations . . . And behold, I am with you always . . ." We love our neighbors and the world as we reach out. In living out his mission, we also connect with Jesus himself.

A life lived in Christ will account for all four inner and outer aspects, not just "my personal relationship with God." Though my relationship with God flows through each, these four give us a bigger gospel vision for what it means to grow spiritually. If we're going to seek to grow in the Christian life, or to help someone else grow, asking some questions in these four categories will help us to identify how to take a meaningful step toward Christ.

These are not abstract concepts, but tangible ways of understanding how you can be nourished by Christ's love and bear

Christ's fruit of love in your life. This vision of spiritual health takes time. Growth doesn't happen overnight. As you place yourself where Jesus is, living in his love, he'll cause you to grow. You simply need to take one step at a time.

Applying the Framework

Now that we have a vision for a bigger gospel approach to the Christian life, we can apply it to spiritual conversations. The bigger gospel approach to the Christian life we just introduced will be utilized for spiritual conversations, but it doesn't tell the whole story. We need a nuanced approach.

At Christ Community Health Services, where we work, we're tasked with engaging in thousands of spiritual conversations every year. It's no surprise, then, that each person we talk to is in a different place spiritually, as well as emotionally, physically, and in their personal maturity. Each person's needs are different. What it looks like to move closer to Jesus is varied for each person. A cookie-cutter approach to evangelism and/or discipleship won't do. What we set out to do here is to give you a framework or flowchart to help guide you in discerning where a person is spiritually.

The goal of your spiritual conversation is to help individuals live out this bigger gospel in their personal life. That can only take place one step at a time. While we want to help them live fully and abundantly in a love relationship with God and according to his design, that goal cannot be fully met in one conversation. While that's what we long to see in ourselves and others, realistically, all we can do is help them to take the next step closer to Jesus. This framework will help you identify with the person what that step might be.

We mentioned in the introduction that the general framework for spiritual conversations is to first understand, and then respond. Let's walk through each aspect of this framework.

First, Understand. Then, Respond.

We first want to listen to individuals and hear what's going on in their lives before we try to suggest any kind of movement toward Jesus. We approach the conversation with our antennae up and ready to receive what the person offers us. You're not trying to force an agenda on a person, but instead you're listening for how God is already at work and seeking to follow after him. That's what Jesus did, isn't it? He said, "Truly, truly, I say to you, the Son can do nothing of his own accord, but only what he sees the Father doing. For whatever the Father does, that the Son does likewise" (John 5:19). In the same way, we can only do what we see the Father doing. We need to ask questions to understand where he's at work so we can follow after.

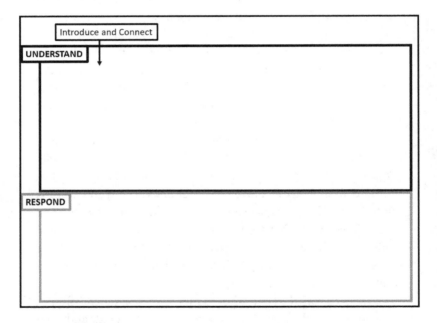

The first step after you've broken the ice and connected as a human being with the other person (introduction) is to seek to understand. By seeking to understand, we mean that you want to take some time to hear what's going on in that person's life. We think the best indicator of what God is doing in someone's life is what that person tells us, rather than what we tell them. If they're sharing with us details about their life, that's our first clue about where God is at work.

On this understanding side, we are first listening to see if someone has a particular care need.

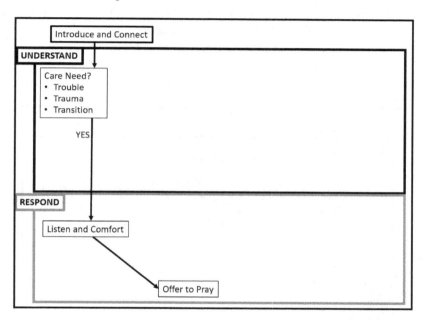

If the answer is yes, then we're only going to listen and comfort that person and ultimately offer to pray with them. Specifically, if someone's dealing with a significant trauma, stressful event, or major transition, then we're not going to try to get them to *do* anything. We think, for the most part, that taking a step toward Jesus for this person is not having a new initiative to "start," but inviting Christ into their situation and seeking to trust him in the midst of it. The goal of the understanding side is to listen, show compassion, and then remind them that God will be with them through it.

Think of your own life. If you've experienced a death, job loss, or cancer diagnosis, you probably felt like you were barely hanging on. Or maybe it was something more positive, like starting a new career, a new degree, or moving to a new city. You needed to receive support in the midst of orienting to your new situation. The essence of this understanding side is listening to what is already occurring in the person's life and sensing God's hand in it. He's at work.

Most of us, however, don't live from stressful event to stressful event. There's a *normal* that we experience. If the person is *not* dealing with a significant care need at that moment in their life, then we want to ask some questions to gauge how receptive the person is to engage in a spiritual conversation and to determine where they are in their spiritual pilgrimage.

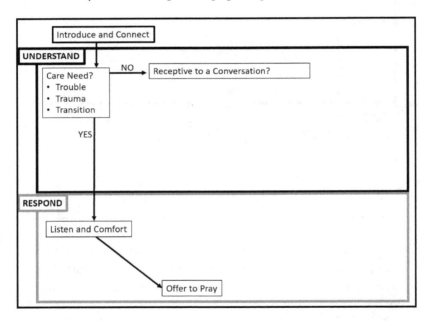

In our conversations with people we don't know well, the first thing we want to do is hear on their own terms where they are in relationship to Christ. Is this person "lost" or not a believer? If so, is this person receptive to hearing more, or are they more closed off? Why? How might God use me to help this person move closer to Christ? What might we be able to say or do to both show respect and at the same time be faithful to what God would have us to do?

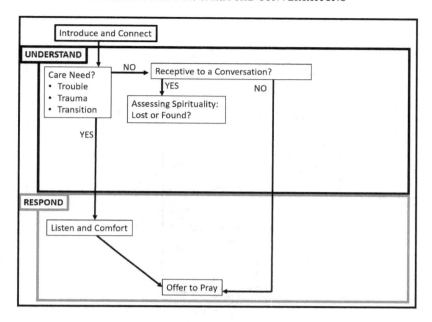

In order to determine the person's relationship to Christ as well as their level of receptivity, we ask some questions that will help us to diagnose the state of their spiritual health. It doesn't do you or the other person any good to try to force something onto them. If they don't seem receptive to a conversation, you can trust that God is still at work, even if it's not the way you may have hoped it would be in that moment. Knowing whether the person is a Christian or not (which we have shortened to "lost" and "found") will determine what proactive step you might take with them. If this person doesn't have a relationship with Jesus (lost), then we'll want to determine if we can help them take a meaningful step toward Christ.

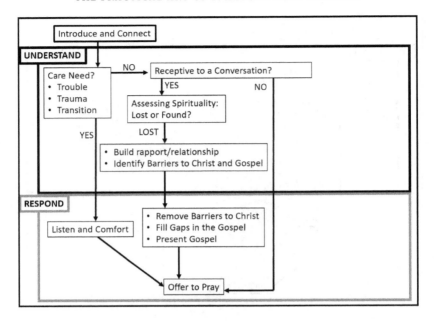

Again, we're still seeking first to understand and trying to learn about the person on their own terms and respect what they're telling us. We want to hear and understand before trying to do anything proactive. And whatever proactive step we might take is largely determined by their level of receptivity. Jesus told his disciples that if someone didn't receive their message, then they could do nothing more in that conversation, and they were to shake the dust off their feet (Matt 10:14, Luke 9:5, Mark 6:11). If there were people who weren't receptive to Jesus' message at that time, then we should suspect that the same will be true in our spiritual conversations as well. Regardless, we want to do what we can to honor the fact that the Lord put us where we are in this moment and do what seems appropriate with this opportunity (Eph 5:16; Col 4:5). We think it's wise to always offer to pray for that person. If God is the one who is ultimately at work, then prayer may be the most powerful thing we can do.

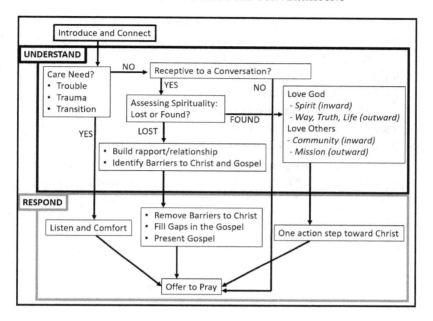

If the person is a Christian (or "found"), then we want to ask some questions in the four areas we introduced when discussing the bigger-gospel approach to the Christian life. As we ask questions in these four areas, we want to help the person articulate one action step they might like to take toward Christ. Their desire to take a step is an indicator of where God might be at work. If we're fallen people with a natural proclivity toward sin (Jer 17:9), then when we desire something that moves us closer to Jesus, it's an indicator of his good work in us (Phil 2:13). So, we listen with an ear to hear where God is at work.

Even the act of answering questions and taking an honest assessment of our life in Christ is a step. It will take a step of courage for the person to share with you openly. The end goal, of course, is to help them move closer to Jesus. But we don't want to diminish the act of sharing.

At the end of every conversation we offer to pray. There's power in prayer. The power isn't in us, but in the work of God in and through us. We offer prayer to acknowledge that this is his work and that we depend on him. There may be exceptions to offering prayer, but by and large we offer to pray. And in our context, 97 percent of the time people take you up on the offer to pray, even if they don't share your beliefs. If the person doesn't want to pray, we don't take offense. We offer it as a gift.

This is our framework for having spiritual conversations. There's an art and a science to it. We'll attempt to teach you both. Regardless, as you seek to love God and love others in your conversations, he'll use you. Continue this journey of growth in learning how to apply this framework well and with wisdom.

4

Who Cares?

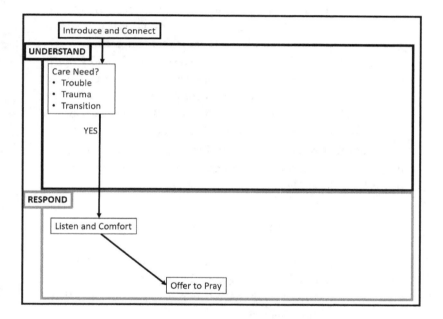

NOT LONG AGO, A young female patient came into one of our medical clinics for an STD screening. This is not uncommon in our clinics. Now imagine that the medical provider enters the room determined to share the gospel with this patient. After all, the physician's assumptions regarding her medical diagnosis might lead him to think that she's not living the Christian life. Out of a heart for evangelism, the physician begins to explain how God loves her, but that she's sinful and separated from God. I mean, that's the gospel, right? But before he even gets to that beautifully crucial bit of a gospel presentation about forgiveness, the girl breaks down into heaving tears. "Can you tell me why you're crying?" the doctor asks. It takes a few seconds to find her voice. But when she does, she says, "I was raped." She weeps inconsolably. It's then that the doctor realizes this may not have been the best moment to present the gospel.

A story like this feels like a theological disconnect for the eager evangelist. Can we really say there's a wrong time to share the gospel? In our opinion, yes, there is a wrong time to share the gospel with someone. But this will require some nuancing.

Let's first say that you should always trust the Holy Spirit's prompting. If you feel led to share the gospel, then err on the side of being faithful, and share. We're not presenting hard-and-fast rules here. We don't think those rules exist. But we can adopt wisdom in the ways we act toward unbelievers (Col 4:5). Is this the exact moment someone needs to hear the gospel? Possibly, yes. But, in general, the wiser way might be to wait until the person is ready. How do we decide?

Shining the Light

One of Jesus' most memorable metaphors proves helpful here. As Christians, we're called to shine Christ's light (Matt 5:14–15; John 8:12; Eph 5:8). However, there's a way of shining our light that is blinding rather than helpful.

I (Jim) have a toddler who loves to play with flashlights. He runs around with his flashlight on, shining it on everything he can. Often, that means shining the light right into my eyes so that it takes them a few minutes to adjust back to normal. His use of the flashlight isn't helpful. I'm convinced that Christians can shine the light of Christ in similar ways—ways that blind rather than illuminate.

Think of the girl who came to our clinic. She'd been raped. She wasn't in a place to see the truth and goodness of the gospel because of the trauma still fresh in her mind. Often in trauma, the visions of the event are so vivid that unless they're dealt with therapeutically, the person experiencing the event can't accurately hear with objectivity and openness. Until love comes in and gives a new vision, one can't see as one should see. This girl didn't have eyes to see. She could only see the trauma of the rape.

Certainly, God can use even the worst of all tragedies to save a person. But we need not assume that's what he's doing at this particular moment. We believe that often the best indicator of what God's doing in someone's life is what the person tells us rather than what we tell them. In order to respond to someone in accordance with the way God is moving in their life, we need to slow down and listen. As we do, we earn the right to speak into their lives.

As a rule, if someone's dealing with a significant trauma, stressful event, or major challenge, then presenting the plan of salvation may not be the most appropriate approach at that time. Just like a hungry person may need food before hearing the gospel, a hurting person may need compassion before hearing the gospel. Listening instead of speaking shows we care, which we think is the greatest need in this kind of interaction. As Col 3:12 reminds us, those who've been chosen by God must be full of compassion and gentleness. As ambassadors of Christ (2 Cor 5:20), people will interpret what God is like through our actions. The reality is that if we come off as uncaring, then it's very likely the person with whom we desire to share will think that the God we serve is also uncaring.

The Music of the Gospel

Here's a way to think about it. Joe Aldrich in his book *Lifestyle Evangelism* writes about the need to join the *words* of the gospel with the *music* of the gospel:

> The words of the gospel are to be incarnated before they are verbalized. The music of the gospel must precede the words of the gospel and prepare the context in which there will be a hunger for those words. What is the music of the gospel? The music of the gospel is the beauty of

the indwelling Christ as lived out in the everyday relationships of life. The gospel is the good news that Jesus
Christ has solved the problem of man's sin and offers him
the potential of an exchanged life, a life in which the resources of God himself are available for his transforma-
tion. And as the gospel is translated into music, it makes
redemptive relationships possible.[1]

People can hear the music of the gospel in several ways. Some
people may already be ready to hear the words of the gospel due
to previous life experiences or encounters with other Christians
before meeting us. In general, however, most people will need to
experience something of the music of the gospel before they're
open to truly consider the claims of the words of the gospel. No
matter when we encounter people, no matter where they are, it's
our job to attune to them. We need to hear the music of their lives
so that we might help them hear the music of the gospel.

When Kelly and I (David) were new missionaries in Spain,
one Sunday afternoon we heard a crashing sound and the screech
of a car fleeing the scene of a hit-and-run accident that turned
out to be someone who'd hit our car that was parked in front of
our house. Our Spanish neighbors, Pedro and Isabel, who lived
directly in front of us, had witnessed the accident and were able
to identify the vehicle of the culprit. They volunteered to help
us file a police report and to cooperate with the investigation.
The important point is that this opened up an opportunity for us
to be on the receiving end of deeds of kindness and generosity
rather than the giving end.

In our experience, putting yourself in the situation of letting
others serve and minister to you often helps to break down walls of
suspicion and resistance like almost nothing else can do. We went
on to have a good friendship with this couple over the years. We
invited them to our home for meals, and they invited us to their
home for a hog slaughter and to their farm in order to see their
chickens and other animals. On one of our first conversations,

---

1. Aldrich, *Lifestyle Evangelism*, 19–20.

though, I learned that one of Pedro's hobbies and passions in life was raising and training messenger pigeons.

Though I didn't know the first thing about messenger pigeons, I expressed an interest in learning more. Sensing I was interested in his hobby, a week or so later Pedro offered to give Kelly and me two messenger pigeons and to build a pen on the roof of our house in which to keep them. And so began my adventure in raising messenger pigeons. It didn't end well, as our dog ended up eating one of them, and the other one escaped and didn't return before we were able to train it. But the fact that I had expressed an interest in Pedro's hobby and was willing to participate together with him and allow him to share his hobby with me opened up doors for relationship building, which in turn opened up doors for sharing the gospel.

The process of building relationships in order to share Christ with others can take time and may well involve doing things we might not otherwise do, such as building a pen on the roof of our house in order to raise messenger pigeons. But the effort is well worth it. And it's more and more the way we'll need to operate in order to be successful in sharing Christ with others in the days ahead, whatever our cultural context may be.

Building a Platform

On the basis of my experiences as a cross-cultural missionary, I (David) see my position as Spiritual Health Advisor at Christ Community Health Services as what is commonly known as a missionary platform. The medical services we at Christ Community offer to people give us an opportunity to share the gospel in a way that we couldn't if we didn't have that platform.

How does that apply to you? Not everyone can be a Spiritual Health Advisor, but all of us can look for platforms that allow for gospel conversations. More often than not, the best platforms are those that meet people at some point of felt need in their life. If we're doing something practical for them, they're more open to what we have to say to them about their spiritual life. But we have to be careful. It's not a quid pro quo. We don't buy the right to share Christ with them. We serve freely, expecting nothing in return. But we seek opportunities our service to others gives us to offer the greatest gift of all, the gift of a relationship with God through Jesus. As the Apostle Paul wrote in 2 Cor 4:5, "For what we proclaim is not ourselves, but Jesus Christ as Lord, with ourselves as your servants for Jesus' sake."

What Is Your Motivation?

I (Jim) was an eager evangelist in college. I would stop people randomly on campus to share the gospel. I memorized arguments to overcome objections to trusting in Christ. I even sought out friends and family to tell them about Jesus. All of these things can be good. But God began convicting my heart. The conviction wasn't about sharing the gospel, but about my motivation for sharing the gospel. I was sharing as a way of feeling good about myself. I wanted to feel spiritual or more committed than other Christians. To put it simply, my goal in evangelism was often selfish.

Paul addressed similar evangelists when he was imprisoned for sharing the gospel. He said in Phil 1:15–18,

> *Some indeed preach Christ from envy and rivalry, but others from good will. The latter do it out of love, knowing that I am put here for the defense of the gospel. The former proclaim Christ out of selfish ambition, not sincerely but thinking to afflict me in my imprisonment. What then? Only that in every way, whether in pretense or in truth, Christ is proclaimed, and in that I rejoice.*

Paul is essentially saying, "Hey, even if people have wrong motives in preaching the gospel, I'm just glad the gospel is getting out there!" I agree.

Even though we can rejoice that the gospel is proclaimed even in wrong motives, Paul makes it clear that our gospel drive ought to be love. This is the entire message of 1 Cor 13:1–3, where Paul said,

If I speak in the tongues of men and of angels, but have not love, I am a noisy gong or a clanging cymbal. And if I have prophetic powers, and understand all mysteries and all knowledge, and if I have all faith, so as to remove mountains, but have not love, I am nothing. If I give away all I have, and if I deliver up my body to be burned, but have not love, I gain nothing.

I'm still an eager evangelist. But I'm striving to become a wise and compassionate evangelist rather than an evangelist who speaks out of selfishness and pretense.

Compassion

The word *compassion* simply means "suffering with." You might think of it as *co-passion*, or shared passion. *Passion* is a word that's lost on most of us. We often use *passion* to mean "what I get really excited about." But we use the word *passion* to also talk about the suffering and death of Jesus Christ, or "the passion of Christ." *Passion* comes from a Latin word that means "to suffer." When we show someone compassion, we *co-suffer*, or enter into their suffering with them. Compassion is a ministry of presence. We're present with the hurting as a tangible expression of Christ's presence with them. In this way, we're not telling them about Christ, but we're representing Christ to them. We're living the music of the gospel instead of merely speaking the gospel.

This might seem like a cop-out to the eager evangelist. But remember that the goal isn't necessarily to preach the gospel every time, but to diagnose where someone is and to help the person move closer toward Christ. In this case, God uses us to show the person Christ's presence, which that person may not readily see or seek because of the trauma they face. The goal, then, is to show Christ-like compassion and help them to trust God through their event and see that he's with them. Think about what Paul tells us in 2 Cor 1:3–4, when he says, "Blessed be the God and Father of our Lord Jesus Christ, the Father of mercies and God of all comfort, who comforts us in all our affliction, so that we may be able to comfort those who are in any affliction, with the comfort with which we ourselves are comforted by God." We comfort them with the same comfort we've received from God.

Often, compassion comes from our own experiences. My wife and I (Jim) struggled with infertility. I've been amazed at how sharing the way that God met us in our infertility has comforted those struggling with infertility. There's something beautiful that happens when we open up about God's comfort in our affliction. But many of us haven't had the same struggles or sufferings as others. And even when we have suffered like they have, we've not been in their exact situation or experience. There's a sense in which we don't really understand what anyone is going through, though we certainly should strive to understand. It's in these moments we must trust the Holy Spirit to help us show compassion. As you do, the Holy Spirit may put in your heart or mind something to do or say that you wouldn't have done or said on your own.

It was supposed to be a quick flight home. I (Jim) brought a book and had no intention of getting into a deep conversation with anyone. Yet, the lady next to me started talking almost in spite of me. She had lost her son to a long battle with a terminal illness. Though it had been years, she seemed eager to share about her grief. She talked about the strain it put on her marriage and her family, and she even shared with me the strain it put on her faith. She struggled to understand how God could allow her son to die. As a result, her relationship with God had become distant over time. She was no longer praying or going to church, and she was questioning whether God really existed at all.

My heart went out to her. Frankly, I couldn't blame her for feeling distant from God. He could have healed her son. Her son's story could have been a story of miraculous healing. But, instead, she was left with pixels on paper to remember the son she loved and an empty bed where her son used to sleep. She was left with a huge hole in her heart.

I asked her questions to try to understand. But I had nothing meaningful to say. I didn't even have children at the time. I had no way of understanding what she was going through. There was an unresolved chord in our conversation as we both got quiet. The flight attendants were preparing for landing, and I knew that we were in the final moments in which I would see this woman in this lifetime. I'd already resigned myself to the fact that I didn't have any role in this conversation other than to listen and show compassion. And so I prepared myself to move on with my day.

She said to me, "I guess I've just felt so distant from God since I lost my son—like God doesn't love me."

My heart broke for her at that moment.

Then, as only the Spirit of God can do, words fell out of my mouth (again, almost in spite of me): "You know, I would think that you would have a closer relationship with God than anyone." She perked up a bit with a confused look on her face and said, "How is it that I would be *closer* to God through this?"

It was the type of look that I knew was pregnant with expectation, like, "You'd better not be messing with me!"

I replied with words that again fell out of my mouth: "Well, it seems like you and God share a bond, in that you both know what it's like to lose a son. He gave his one and only Son up to death for you and me. You can relate to God in a special way that I can't. I don't know the type of heartbreak both you and he have experienced."

I watched peace rush into her heart as she said, "I guess I've never thought of it that way."

Well-known pastor Rick Warren lost his son due to suicide. In the midst of this, here's what he said about the God of all comfort: "Your most profound and intimate experiences of worship will likely be in your darkest days—when your heart is broken, when you feel abandoned, when you're out of options, when the pain is great—and you turn to God alone."[2] God can meet people in a special way in the midst of suffering. A broken heart can be the most sacred of cathedrals where God can be known. If we're sensitive to these as would-be evangelists, we may see God work in significant ways that go beyond us. God may be at work in someone who is suffering. If we distract them from what God is doing

2. Warren, *Purpose Driven Life*, 176.

by trying to force our own agenda, though, we may distract them from moving closer to him.

The Art and Science of Compassion

Now let's make this practical. We've shared with you the need to approach spiritual conversations from a framework of first seeking to understand and then respond. Our response to those who are hurting should be compassion. How do we show compassion?

We like to think of compassion as both an art and a science. The art is showing a genuine heart of compassion for the person who is suffering. You can't fake that—because it comes from who you are. But let's face it. Many of us can suffer compassion fatigue or contend with our own struggles, which at times makes it difficult to feel compassion for someone else. In that case, the science of compassion can help us. We can show compassion using practical tools even if we don't feel compassion. Before you think that's heartless, the motivation in showing compassion (even when you don't feel it) is a heart to serve and love the suffering person. Let's talk about both the art and science of compassion.

The Art

The goal in soul care is to show Christ-like compassion and help the one with whom we're talking to trust God through their event and see that he's with them. We listen and suffer with them through whatever they're facing. In this way, we point people to Christ. In order to see people open up to us about their suffering, we first need to be the type of person with whom someone would want to share their suffering.

Think of someone you'd call or to whom you'd open up if you were going through suffering. What is it about that person that might cause you to choose them to share your suffering with? What are those virtues or characteristics about them that encourage you to open up? There's no exhaustive list, but here are a few ingredients we've heard as we've asked people this question.

- Humble—"I'm not better than you."

- Non-judgmental—"I won't judge you or blame you."

- Loving—"I'm committed to you no matter what you tell me."

- Substantial (rather than silly)—"I'll take you seriously."

- Compassionate—"I'll be present with you through this."

- Eager to connect—"I want to hear from you."

- Calming/Peaceful—"I'll not be disturbed by what you share with me."

- Genuine—"I'm interested in you."

- Hopeful—"I'll trust and believe in you."

These can't be faked. In order for people to open up to you, you have to be the type of person to whom someone would want to open up. People are subconsciously watching us all the time to see if we're a "safe" person or not. As you display these characteristics, people will know that they can share with you when they enter into a difficult season. Isn't this the type of person we long to be?

The Science

In addition to these character traits, there are also practical tools that can be used at the moment someone opens up that invite them further into sharing. These are not so much character traits as they are skills that can be developed and deployed regardless of how we feel. Any good counselor or psychologist has learned how to sharpen these skills in order to draw people out. Here are a few of these tools:

- Show interest through non-verbal cues (eye-contact, open posture, same level, tone of voice, appropriate touch)

- Ask questions to understand and draw out—"Tell me more about that."

- Demonstrate understanding through what is said—"I can tell you are hurting."

- Validate feelings and experiences—"It must be so hard to go through this."

- Normalize what's being felt or experienced—"Anyone in your situation would feel the same way."

There are a great many books and resources on how to develop these tools. You can hone and develop these, but here's the deal: You don't have to be a Christian in order to show Christ-like compassion. A non-believer can display the characteristics of a person to whom you'd open up as well as the practical tools necessary to draw people out in the moment of their sharing.

C.A.R.E.

What makes compassion or care distinctively Christian? We believe the difference lies in the fact that the person showing Christian care goes beyond compassion to pointing this person to Christ. How do we point people to Christ in the midst of showing compassion? We C.A.R.E.

> C—Consecrate Christ as Lord
>
> A—Attend to the Spirit and the person
>
> R—Respond with prayer
>
> E—Encourage toward Christ

First, *consecrate Christ as Lord*. First Peter 3:15 reminds us to consecrate Jesus Christ as Lord. It's important that we know Christ leads out in front of anything we do. When we look to have a spiritual conversation with a person, it's important that we remember that Christ has been with this person before us, is with this person now, and will be the one who goes with them after our conversation is complete. Psalm 34:18 reminds us that God is near to the brokenhearted and saves those whose spirit is crushed. We must first remember this before we can effectively point anyone to the present Christ.

Second, we must *attend to the Spirit and the person*. We've already shared how we can attend to the person through the practical tools. While this is good, in order to be led by God, we must be sensitive to the Holy Spirit. Only the Spirit truly knows this person and what we should do. God may prompt you to ask a certain question or he may encourage you to remain silent. The Spirit may nudge you to place a hand on their shoulder, grab for a box of tissues, or hold a hand in prayer. As you know God's voice, you'll sense his leadership in the moment. This requires double-attention as we listen to the person and the Holy Spirit.

Third, we should *respond with prayer*. We want to offer them the Savior before we offer a solution. Often, when someone is hurting, we're quick to try to solve the problem. We'd discourage you from that until you pray for them first. In praying with this person, you'll tangibly express that you're not the savior; instead, you'll bring them before the Savior. God may lay a suggestion on your heart. Offering it after prayer will allow you to further follow the Spirit's leading. In this way, we model faith in Christ on the person's behalf.

Finally, *encourage the person toward Christ*. Many of us believe that God's hand of blessing on us means we'll be free from suffering. When we suffer, we assume that it's a sign of God's absence. A basic reading of Scripture shows us that's not true. It may be that we're even more blessed when we do suffer. It's important to remind people that God hasn't left them nor forsaken them (Deut 31:8; Heb 13:5), even in their suffering. Even if the suffering is due to our own sinful choices, God is still waiting with open arms to receive us back to himself. He promises to draw near to all who draw near to him (Jas 4:8; Ps 145:18). It's never too late to draw near to God.

Understanding Before Responding

We said earlier that we should first seek to understand, and then respond. This chapter has been about the understanding side of a spiritual encounter with someone who's hurting. Before we proactively share with someone, we first want to understand their needs. Most of us are not currently in the middle of a trauma or life-changing difficulty—so once we determine that this person isn't in the middle of such a significant event, we can move toward becoming more proactive in our effort to point people to Christ.

Francis Schaeffer once said, "If I have only an hour with someone, I will spend the first fifty-five minutes asking questions and finding out what is troubling their heart and mind, and then in the last five minutes I will share something of the truth."[3] While you may be eager to get to the responding side of this framework, the rule of listening first should not fade to the background. In fact, much of this book is motivated by teaching you how to listen and discern where someone is spiritually. As we do, we can better point people to Christ.

3. Jerram Barrs, "Francis Schaeffer," para. 64.

---- 5 ----

From Lost to Found

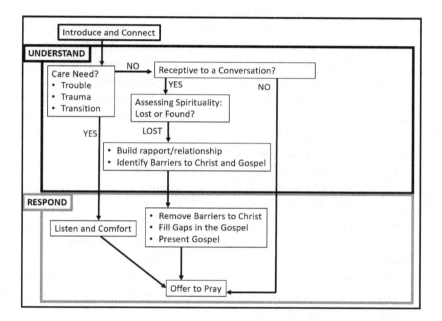

MARATHON TRAINING MAY BE harder than the actual marathon. As part of the training, you increase the distance you run each day. It becomes a part-time job just to get all the miles in each week. I (Jim) remember one specific training run when my task was to run fifteen miles. I liked to run on a high school track because I didn't have to worry about traffic or tripping on uneven sidewalks. Because of the repetition of quarter-mile laps, it was difficult to remember which mile and even which lap I was on. In order to keep track (pun intended), I carried pennies that equaled the number of miles I'd run for that day. On this particular day, there was a table next to the track, so I'd place one penny on the table each time I completed a mile. Obviously, over the course of fifteen miles my body began to break down and get tired. Around mile eleven I was ready to quit. At mile thirteen, I thought I was going to pass out. Finally, I finished mile fifteen. I victoriously passed the table and put the final penny on it as I passed by with excitement.

I walked around to catch my breath and to loosen up my weary legs. After doing so, I started making my way back to the table to grab my pennies. As I picked them up, I counted each one with pride. But there was a problem. There were only fourteen pennies. I started looking around to find the fifteenth penny. Surely, it fell off the table! I searched the ground, the table, and the track, but found no penny. I thought to myself, "What if I only ran fourteen miles? That would mean I'm not done and still have another mile to go. I don't think I can do another mile now." Frantically, I began to search even harder. I desperately wanted to find that penny.

Why was I concerned about that penny? I didn't need the penny. I could easily pay my bills if I never found the penny. It wasn't because it was valuable. I had a whole jar of pennies at home. I desperately wanted to find that penny because it represented the sacrifice and exertion of a mile. It had value to me because I worked hard to put that penny on the table. I ended up finding the penny. And I must have looked like a crazy person, smiling and celebrating because I found one measly penny.

Jesus tells a similar story in Luke 15:8–10: "Or what woman, having ten silver coins, if she loses one coin, does not light a lamp and sweep the house and seek diligently until she finds it? And when she has found it, she calls together her friends and neighbors, saying, 'Rejoice with me, for I have found the coin that I had lost.' Just so, I tell you, there is joy before the angels of God over one sinner who repents."

What was lost has been found! This is cause for celebration. When we think about our participation in God's work of saving lost souls, Jesus' heart toward the lost guides us. *Lost* implies something that was previously possessed by the owner. A person who comes to salvation in Christ is simply returning to God what is rightfully his. We're not valuable on our own. We're just dust (Ps 103:14). What gives us value is who owns us. What gives us value is what Christ has sacrificed for us. What gives us value is God's image stamped upon us. Like my running pennies, we're only valuable as God's possession. When we invite someone to the gospel of Jesus Christ and salvation in him, we're returning what was lost back to God.

Salvation: A Relationship with Jesus

Earlier, we contrasted the big gospel with the small gospel. Our goal was to say that the gospel is so much bigger than one's personal salvation. The gospel is bigger because it impacts the whole universe. The gospel is God's activity of returning everything in the universe back to him and his ways, not just saving *me*. While the gospel is so much more than personal salvation, it is not less. It's still true that people need personal salvation in Christ. The foundation for living as God designed is a personal relationship with him.

If someone asked you how they can have a personal relationship with God, what might you say? This might feel like a remedial question for someone who picked up a book like this, but we've learned not to take this for granted. We've asked this question to people who've been serving in ministry for years, some of whom have doctorates in ministry, and have gotten very vague answers. We've asked this question to devout Christians and church leaders, and we've often found that those asked can't articulate what it means to enter into the most foundational and important relationship in the universe. So how do we introduce someone to a relationship with Jesus Christ? The main contours are simple enough.

The goal: a relationship with God.

God designed you to have a relationship with him. Jesus said that he came to give you a thriving and meaningful life (John 10:10). As we live in a loving relationship with God, we experience life and peace. A Christian is someone who lives in a loving relationship with God (John 17:3).

The problem: separation from God.

Being in a relationship with God is not automatic. God is completely perfect and holy. All humans make mistakes and fail to live up to God's perfect standard. When we fail, it's called *sin*. The Bible says, ". . . for all have sinned and fall short of the glory of God" (Rom 3:23). Our sin separates us from a relationship with God (Rom 6:23).

The cure: Jesus Christ!

God's love bridges the gap of separation between you and him. Jesus Christ died on the cross to forgive our sin. He then rose from the dead. And this makes it possible for us to have a new life. The Bible says, "[Jesus] himself bore our sins in his body on the tree, that we might die to sin and live to righteousness. By his wounds you have been healed" (1 Pet 2:24). It is only through Jesus Christ that you can be forgiven of sin and have a relationship with God.

How do I become a Christian?

You cross the bridge into a relationship with God when you turn away from your sin, believe in Christ, and receive his free gift of salvation. The Bible says, "But to all who did receive him, who believed in his name, he gave the right to become children of God" (John 1:12). When you receive Christ, you become a child of God and are accepted into his family.

What do I do?

Admit you have failed to live up to God's perfect standard. Ask God to forgive you and turn away from your sin. Believe that Christ died on the cross for you and rose from the dead. Begin your relationship with God today. Romans 10:13 says, "For everyone who calls on the name of the Lord will be saved."

Here's a prayer you can pray to receive Christ:

"Dear Lord Jesus, I know that I'm a sinner, and I ask for your forgiveness. I believe that you died for my sins and rose from the dead. I turn from my sin and trust and follow you as my Lord and Savior. Guide my life and help me as I begin my new relationship with you. In Jesus' name, amen."

Tailoring Your Approach

Of course, there's much more that can be added and a variety of ways we could present how to have a relationship with Jesus Christ. The most important thing, though, is to actually do the work of telling the lost how they can be found in Christ. The style of presentation depends on the person to whom you're speaking. It will require you to listen to them to know best how to share.

We need to be thoughtful about the types of words we use when discussing spiritual things. Words like *sin* and *forgiveness* take on a different meaning than they have in decades past. We can't assume that people understand what's meant by those words. Even those who call themselves Christians may not have an actual understanding of the gospel nor certain key elements for understanding it. So, though the message of the gospel is clear, the presentation will vary.

How might we frame the gospel for people who don't readily understand the words we've traditionally used to explain it? Here we can learn from Paul. Paul preached the gospel very differently at a secular Mars Hill (Acts 17) than he did in the synagogue (Acts

13). He built bridges to his audience's understanding using symbols and words that would have been meaningful to them. He didn't talk about the history of the nation of Israel, like those seeking to share Christ with people from a Jewish background often did on other occasions in the New Testament. Rather, Paul referenced Greek philosophers and Greek religious practices. He called out the falsehood in their beliefs by contrasting them with the true God, but he did so in a way that resonated with his hearers. He invited them to turn away from their wrong ways and toward a right relationship with God, but in a loving and winsome way. The point is that he tailored his approach to what would be meaningful to the audience without compromising the truth of the message.

Mistaken Gospels

While it's often helpful, and indeed needful, to tailor our approach for the audience to whom we're speaking, we must be careful that it's our approach we are tailoring and not the gospel message itself. Paul in Gal 1:6–7 warned against turning to a different gospel—which is really no gospel at all. There are a number of ways we may think we understand the gospel but at the same time fail to grasp it as it truly is. We don't wish to offer an exhaustive list here, but we do want to offer a few ways many can miss the gospel.

The "Ticket-to-Heaven" Gospel

First, if your bottom-line goal is simply to get to heaven when you die, then you may not have truly accepted Christ at all. Salvation is not primarily a ticket to heaven. Salvation is about a relationship with God. The word the Bible uses to describe this relationship is *reconciliation*. We're reconciled to him, which means we're no longer a "child of wrath" but are now a "child of God." We're adopted into God's family. These are relational terms that have to do with our status before God. A view that emphasizes heaven makes salvation sound more like a vacation than a relationship. This view misconstrues the goal. The primary goal is not the destination but the relationship. Even the way we think about heaven can confuse what salvation is. Life after death is not merely about vacating to another place, but about God making his everlasting home with humanity, both in heaven and on earth. In Rev 21:3, God says, "Behold, the dwelling place of God is with man. He will dwell with them, and they will be his people, and God himself will be with them as their God." The goal of salvation is not merely forgiveness, nor heaven, but living in a perfect relationship with God forever.

The "Earn-It-Yourself" Gospel

Another way we can misinterpret the gospel is to think we have to do something to earn it. Think about yourself in your darkest moment, when you've sinned most destructively. How does God view you? If you consider yourself a Christian, but your answer is with disappointment or shame, then there's a part of you that doesn't truly believe the good news of Jesus Christ. Romans 8:1 says that there's now no condemnation for all those who are in Christ Jesus. When we accept God's free gift of grace in our lives, we pass from a state of being under God's wrath to a state of being under God's mercy (Eph 2:1–5).

There are many who try to do all the right things in order to earn God's approval. It's an approach to faith that assumes that if you go to church or read your Bible and pray or give 10 percent of your money to God, then he'll be pleased with you and love you. The converse of this approach is the idea that if you don't do those things, then God will be disappointed or reject you. The reality is that we all fail to live up to God's perfect standard. We should strive for holiness and to live according to God's ways, but this should be fueled by gratitude rather than a desire to earn approval. In Rom 12:1 we're told that it's in view of God's mercies that we offer ourselves to God. We don't offer ourselves for any other reason than gratitude for the grace and mercy God has already shown us in Christ Jesus.

The "Just-Say-the-Magic-Words" Gospel

Another way we may misinterpret the gospel is by thinking we enter into a relationship with God by means of a simple prayer in which we say some "magic words" and now we're saved. Now it's totally true that, as we've already said, we're saved by grace alone through faith alone in Christ alone. In other words, there's absolutely nothing we can do to earn our salvation. In the end, our new relationship with God begins as a result of something that happens inside of us, in our hearts, and not through something we say or do.

This something that happens inside us is what the Bible calls *faith*. Now when we say the word *faith*, we generally think of believing something to be true. But true biblical faith isn't mere mental assent to a set of propositions. James 2:19 says, "You believe that God is one; you do well. Even the demons believe—and shudder!" The faith that opens the door for us to begin our relationship with God and eventually make it to heaven is a faith that comes from the heart. Someone once said that some people are going to miss out on heaven—and on their relationship with God—by eighteen inches. The eighteen inches they were talking about is the typical distance between someone's head and their heart. The following illustration helps to explain the difference between merely believing with your head and believing with your heart.

In the summer of 1859, to the amazement of a crowd of 25,000 spectators, the world-renowned tightrope walker Charles Blondin walked across a rope stretched across Niagara Falls. As the story goes, after crossing from the American side to the Canadian side with a pole to help to balance himself, and then back across from the Canadian side to the American side without the pole, he announced to the spectators gathered on the American side that he was going to cross a third time, only this time he was going to do it pushing a wheelbarrow in front of him. As he prepared to make the crossing, he asked the crowd, "Who believes that I can make it across with the wheelbarrow?" And the crowd wildly cheered their assent. Then he pointed to a man in the crowd and said, "You, sir, if you really believe I can do it, go ahead and get in the wheelbarrow."

Though Blondin eventually did carry a man on his back across Niagara Falls, and on another occasion, he made the crossing pushing a wheelbarrow, there's no record of him ever pushing someone across the falls in a wheelbarrow. The point of the story, though, is that there's one kind of faith that is the faith of the crowd gathered along the shores of Niagara Falls cheering their assent, saying they believe, and then there's the faith of the person who's willing to get in the wheelbarrow and entrust their life in the hands of the one pushing. True, life-giving faith in Christ is the type of faith in which we as Christ's followers place ourselves in the metaphorical wheelbarrow he's pushing across the Niagara Falls of life.

Upon hearing this story, we may despair, thinking we could never have such a great faith as this. But as J. Hudson Taylor famously said, "You do not need a great faith, but faith in a great God."[1] Jesus said that if we only have faith as a grain of mustard seed, we can say to a mountain, "Be cast into the sea," and it will obey us (Matt 17:20; Luke 17:6). But true, authentic, saving faith involves yielding the control of our life over to the Master Wheelbarrow-Pusher, Jesus. It's not by our works, or even our "magic words." We, by our own effort, could never hope to make it safely across on our own. It is all by his power and his grace alone. But in order to benefit from his power and grace, we've first got to express our faith in him by placing ourselves in the wheelbarrow. And it's impossible to stay with one foot on the sideline and one foot in the wheelbarrow. We've got to be all in.

We may not completely understand all the implications of surrendering our lives to Jesus when we take that first step of faith. Indeed, the more we walk with Jesus, the more we'll become increasingly aware of our own shortcomings and failures. But the Bible doesn't present an Option A (just praying the prayer and getting your ticket to heaven) and an Option B (full-fledged discipleship) when it describes the process of evangelism. Though our understanding of all the implications of faith may—and must—grow deeper as time goes on, authentic salvation involves

1. Steer, *Hudson Taylor*, 51.

giving all we know of ourselves to all we know of Christ at the moment we believe.

Spiritual Diagnosis

In the book *What's Gone Wrong with the Harvest?* James F. Engel presents a model for thinking about evangelism and growth in our relationship with Christ that has come to be known as the Engel Scale.[2]

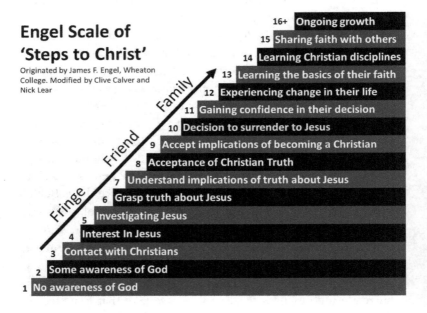

Engel Scale of 'Steps to Christ'

Originated by James F. Engel, Wheaton College. Modified by Clive Calver and Nick Lear

Family
Friend
Fringe

16+ Ongoing growth
15 Sharing faith with others
14 Learning Christian disciplines
13 Learning the basics of their faith
12 Experiencing change in their life
11 Gaining confidence in their decision
10 Decision to surrender to Jesus
9 Accept implications of becoming a Christian
8 Acceptance of Christian Truth
7 Understand implications of truth about Jesus
6 Grasp truth about Jesus
5 Investigating Jesus
4 Interest In Jesus
3 Contact with Christians
2 Some awareness of God
1 No awareness of God

Though there are many possible ways to describe the steps to growth in our relationship to Christ, the scale above provides one graphic portrayal of the steps someone may pass through not only on their way to believing and embracing the good news of salvation (Steps 1–10) but also in their subsequent growth as a follower of Jesus (Steps 11–16).

2. Engel and Norton, *What's Gone Wrong with the Harvest?*, 45.

Several important observations are in order. First of all, Christian growth begins way back at Step 2 and continues all the way up to Step 16. This means that some type of spiritual encounter is appropriate for anyone and everyone, no matter at what stage along the Engel Scale they may happen to find themselves at that particular time. Another important observation is that growth in our relationship with Christ normally occurs little by little, step by step, rather than by giant leaps. For instance, it may not be the best strategy to try to move someone from, say, Step 2 all the way to Step 10 in one conversation. It may be more helpful, rather, to attempt to move them from, say, Step 3 to Step 4. The approach we take with each individual will vary in accord with where they presently fall on the Engel Scale, the amount of time we have to spend with them, and their current degree of receptivity and readiness to progress further along in their spiritual growth.

A Different Approach to Spiritual Conversations

This is a very different approach to spiritual conversations than what many of us are used to. Many of us have been trained to share a canned gospel presentation. While we believe it's important to have a variety of tools (canned gospel presentations) ready to share when the time is right, many of us have failed in our attempts to have a meaningful spiritual conversation with someone because we had the wrong goal. If the goal is to simply present the plan of salvation, we may miss a great opportunity to help move someone closer to Christ. When our only goal is to share the plan of salvation, opportunities seem sparse (especially in the Bible Belt, where we live). And when we do talk about spiritual things with someone, it often feels superficial. What we're presenting in this book means we can't treat every person the same.

We must listen, understand, and try to spiritually discern where this person is currently at and what we may be able to do, given the time and situation at hand, to help them move one step closer toward full maturity in Christ. How we share our faith will reveal what we think it actually means to be a Christian and therefore what we think the goal of spirituality is. What we share with someone in the spiritual conversation is some aspect of a vision for the Christian life. If something is off there, it will not just impact our interactions, but our own lives as well. The goal then is not just to introduce the plan of salvation, but to help that person take the next step—whatever that may be—toward living fully under Christ's lordship.

Matthew 28:18–20, popularly known as the Great Commission, says that we as Christ's followers are to make disciples of all nations by means of a two-fold process: First, baptizing them in the name of the Father, the Son, and the Holy Spirit—in other words, helping them to repent and believe, enter into a new relationship with the Holy Trinity, and identify with the Body of Christ. Next, teaching them to obey all the things he commands us to do as his disciples. In other words, the Great Commission involves helping people to *become* Christians and also helping people to *be* Christians. Our ultimate objective as disciple-makers is not just getting them to cross the line of knowing that when they die they will go to heaven, but also to teach people to live a life of intimate fellowship with Jesus and faithful obedience to Jesus up until that time comes.

A model of evangelism that focuses on helping people to cross the starting line of a relationship with Christ but then leaves them there at that starting line without actually running the race is a truncated evangelism that may actually short-circuit their arrival at the finish line. Some people think, "Well, just as long as I get them across the starting line, I've done my part. Someone else can come in later and bring them further along. At least, the most important work of making sure they will make it to heaven when they die has been accomplished." But, in actuality, this model of evangelism may (at best) produce unhealthy and unproductive disciples of Christ, or (at worst) lead people to trust in walking an aisle, saying a prayer, signing a card, and thinking they are saved, without ever truly having experienced a life-changing, soul-saving relationship with Jesus Christ.

A more biblical and holistic approach to evangelism sees what's often called *evangelism* and what's often called *discipleship* as part of the same process. When we have the end-goal in mind—to present everyone fully mature in Christ (Col 1:28)—it will affect the way we approach the evangelistic process from start to finish. Some techniques that may be useful in the short run to get people to verbally assent to what we are saying or to say a prayer to ask Jesus to come into their heart may ultimately prove to be counterproductive in helping those same people reach full maturity in Christ.

Christian musician Keith Green wrote about the danger of inducing spiritual abortions by rushing the process of the Holy Spirit's work in someone's life and pressuring them to make a decision for Christ and sign on the dotted line, as it were, before they've truly counted the cost and understood the demands of discipleship.[3] When the Pharisees and Sadducees came to John the Baptist and asked to be baptized, he told them to come back when they could produce "fruit in keeping with repentance" (Matt 3:8). Jesus on various occasions advised people to count the cost of discipleship before following him (Matt 10:37–39, 19:16–21; Luke 14:25–33).

We need not feel pressure to see a dramatic result from our spiritual conversations. Sometimes the progress is little by little. Often the conversations we have are only one step along the way in a person's pilgrimage toward Christ. This approach, however, frees us up to see *every* conversation we have with someone else, no matter who they are, and no matter how short or how long, as an opportunity to bring that person one step further along the path on their pilgrimage toward Christ! We may not have time during a brief transaction with a salesclerk at the convenience store to lay out the full plan of salvation. But somewhere along the way in our interaction with them we can make them aware that we are Christians and try to do or say something, however insignificant it may seem at the time, that might spark an interest in that person to know more about faith in Christ. Even if

3. Green, "What's Wrong with the Gospel?"

it becomes evident that person already has a relationship with Christ, we will want to do something or say something in our brief (or extended) encounter that will stir them up to love and good works (Heb 10:24) and will help them to take that next step forward in their relationship with Christ.

As we plant gospel seeds in someone else's life, we also need to remember that evangelism is a team activity. In John 4:38–39, Jesus says, "For here the saying holds true, 'One sows and another reaps.' I sent you to reap that for which you did not labor. Others have labored, and you have entered into their labor." The truth of the matter is that God gifts each of us with different personalities and different skills. Some are better at sowing, others at cultivating, and others at reaping. But we're all part of the same team that God uses to bring somebody to faith in Christ.

In this chapter, we've presented a broad overview of the gospel message we seek to communicate, along with some key concepts that influence our general approach toward introducing someone to a relationship with Christ. While the core gospel message we present will always be the same, it's important to recognize that different people have different obstacles that get in the way of them coming to faith in Christ and different levels of receptivity to our efforts to help them understand and embrace the gospel. In the next chapter, we'll continue the journey of equipping you to share new life in Christ with all kinds of people by focusing more closely on the issues of obstacles and receptivity.

$$6$$

Obstacles to the Gospel and Receptivity

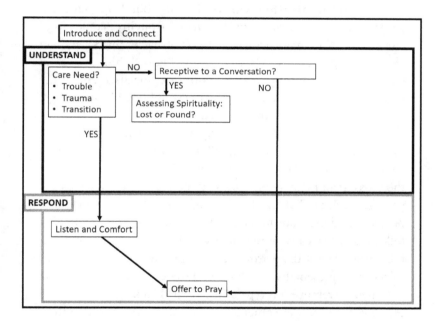

IN THE LAST CHAPTER, we discussed evangelism as one step in a larger spectrum of discipleship. In doing so, we suggested that there may be many steps a person needs to take before actually entering into a relationship with Jesus Christ. In this chapter, we'll consider what some of those obstacles might be and how in our spiritual conversations we might faithfully clear the way for people to enter into a relationship with Jesus Christ.

Clearing Obstacles

One of the most helpful models of effective evangelism/discipleship is that of identifying and removing obstacles in people's lives that are keeping them from taking the next step toward a fuller and more faithful relationship with Christ. The prophet Isaiah, in the midst of his prophetic call for God's people to return to their faithful relationship with God, said, "Build up, build up, prepare the way, remove every obstruction from my people's way" (Isa 57:14). With many people, there are obstacles that keep them from coming to faith in Christ and walking with him in faithful obedience in their daily lives. As faithful evangelists, one of the main tasks we have is to clear away the stumbling blocks that get in the way of people's faith and obedience.

We must be careful to distinguish between the offense of the gospel itself and other stumbling blocks that we as humans sometimes add to the gospel. The gospel itself—or the message of the cross—can be an offense or a stumbling block for people, as passages such as 1 Pet 2:7–8 and 1 Cor 1:18 make clear. Sometimes people just don't want to let go of their sin and they know that following Christ calls for repentance and self-sacrifice. Sometimes their pride keeps them from recognizing they can't save themselves. As representatives of Jesus and sharers of the gospel, we're *not* called to remove this type of stumbling block.

But then there are other stumbling blocks that are not inherent in the gospel itself, that we put up by the things we say, by our attitudes, by our bad testimony, or by adding requirements to the gospel that are really just our cultural preferences and not true gospel essentials. The Bible has some very strong words of warning about these types of stumbling blocks and the need to do everything possible to avoid hindering people coming to Christ and giving them an excuse not to believe the gospel. The Apostle Paul, speaking of his decision to not solicit financial support for his ministry from the Christians in Corinth, said, "We endure anything rather than put an obstacle in the way of the gospel of Christ" (1 Cor 9:12b).

The truth is, we currently live in a time in which there are many stumbling blocks for the effective communication of the gospel in the world all around us. Sadly, there are hypocrites, who by the inconsistency of their lifestyles make it difficult for people to hear the message about Christ with an open mind. Differences about approaches to politics, and especially the strident tone with which we communicate them, often cause people to close their minds to the message of grace and forgiveness that we are seeking to share with them. Selfishness and indifference on the part of Christians toward the needs and concerns of the people around them often create another barrier that gets in the way of people hearing the gospel with an open heart and open mind.

In addition to the stumbling blocks that we ourselves may put up that get in the way of people coming to Christ, there are often other obstacles that keep people from surrendering their lives to him. One of the most important aspects of effective evangelism involves seeking to identify these obstacles and then directing our efforts, through our spiritual conversations, toward overcoming them. In order to do this, we must first identify the particular obstacles in the path of the person to whom we are speaking.

Intellectual Obstacles

Some people have intellectual questions that keep them from believing: Why does evil exist? What is the purpose of suffering in the world? Isn't the Bible full of contradictions? Aren't we all just the products of evolution anyway? Isn't the God of the Old Testament a cruel tyrant who commands genocide and slaughters children?

In order to clear away these rocks and stones, it will sometimes be necessary to listen sincerely and attentively to what the people asking these questions are *really* saying. Although it helps to spend some time studying and thinking through the best responses to the most common intellectual questions people have, it's important to humbly admit that we're never going to be fully prepared to answer every question to everyone's satisfaction. However, our willingness to at least listen and take seriously what others are saying goes a long way toward breaking down barriers.

Emotional Obstacles

For other people, the rocks and stones obscuring their pathway of faith may not be intellectual questions but, rather, emotional issues. At some point in their life, someone who claimed to be a Christian may have wounded them in some way or another. For valid or invalid reasons, they may perceive the public advocates of Christianity as self-serving hypocrites. Some personal trauma or life-altering experience may preoccupy their emotional energy to such a degree that they're unable to give full attention to the gospel message and be saved. People like this will likely need to be exposed to a greater dose of the music of the gospel before they're ready to hear the words of the gospel.

Cultural Obstacles

For other people, the rocks and stones on their pathway may be cultural. They may perceive the gospel we're proclaiming as relevant for people from other cultural backgrounds, but not for them. It's for this reason that Paul said what he said in 1 Cor 9:19–22:

> *For though I am free from all, I have made myself a servant to all, that I might win more of them. To the Jews I became as a Jew, in order to win Jews. To those under the law I became as one under the law (though not being myself under the law) that I might win those under the law. To those outside the law I became as one outside the law (not being outside the law of God but under the law of Christ) that I might win those outside the law. To the weak I became weak, that I might win the weak. I have become all things to all people, that by all means I might save some.*

It would be a lot easier to share the gospel with people if everyone came from the same background and shared the same cultural presuppositions. But in the diverse world in which we live, this is often not the case. Because of this reality, those who have little access to the gospel will need someone who is willing to cross geographical, linguistic, and cultural barriers in order for them to hear the message of salvation in a way that makes sense to them. That's a big part of what cross-cultural missionaries do. In the same way, though, we as evangelists right here at home must be sensitive to the cultural presuppositions of those with whom we share the gospel. We must seek to present the message from beginning to end. At every point along the Engel Scale, in ways that make sense to them and don't raise unnecessary cultural obstacles to the universal, we must seek to the transcultural message of God's grace through faith in Christ.

Spiritual Obstacles

Another common obstacle we'll face when trying to communicate the gospel to others is spiritual blindness. Paul says in 2 Cor 4:3–4, "And even if our gospel is veiled, it is veiled to those who are perishing. In their case the god of this world has blinded the minds of the unbelievers, to keep them from seeing the light of the gospel of the glory of Christ, who is the image of God." When we think about it, this is a serious obstacle! The Bible says these people are literally unable to correctly perceive the light of the gospel! Satan has blinded them!

If this is the case, our efforts to share the gospel may at first appear to be a lost cause. How can we ever get through to these people if Satan has blinded them so they can't see the truth? But the Bible gives us hope to overcome the spiritual barrier. Paul said to King Agrippa in Acts 26:17–18 that Jesus told him when he called him to proclaim the gospel, "I am sending you to the Gentiles to open their eyes, so they may turn from darkness to light and from the power of Satan to God." But the only way we can overcome spiritual obstacles is with spiritual weapons. Paul says in 2 Cor 10:3–5, "We are human, but we don't wage war as humans do. We use God's mighty weapons, not worldly weapons, to knock down the strongholds of human reasoning and to destroy false arguments. We destroy every proud obstacle that keeps people from knowing God. We capture their rebellious thoughts and teach them to obey Christ" (NLT).

Among the spiritual weapons we're given to wage war as we share the gospel with spiritually blinded people are the weapons of prayer and fasting (Matt 17:21) and pleading the power of the blood of Jesus in the context of self-sacrificial boldness: "And they have defeated him [i.e., Satan] by the blood of the Lamb and by their testimony. And they did not love their lives so much that they were afraid to die" (Rev 12:11).

Tools in Your Toolbox

Each person with whom we talk and with whom we develop a relationship is going to have a different set of obstacles that's getting in the way of them taking the next step toward faith in Christ or maturity in Christ. Because of this, we must constantly listen to what they're saying and allow the Holy Spirit to direct the approach we should take in each individual case. Even though the particular obstacles each individual with whom we engage in spiritual conversation may be unique to that individual, there are certain tools in our evangelism toolbox that remain the same.

There are attitudes like love and compassion that we ought to manifest in every situation. And no matter whom we're talking with and no matter the situations in their life, we must always rely on the power and guidance of the Holy Spirit. While there is indeed a certain art and science behind effective evangelism and discipleship, we ought to remember that these are spiritual tasks that depend on the power and guidance of the Holy Spirit.

Another key tool in our toolbox is our knowledge and use of the Bible. It's good to have a certain set of verses that we've memorized that help us to explain the basics of the gospel. But beyond this, it's good to cultivate a working knowledge of the principles of Scripture and a good understanding of how they apply to real-life circumstances of the people with whom we're conversing. In Matt 13:52, Jesus told his disciples, "Every student of the Scriptures who becomes a disciple in the kingdom of heaven is like someone who brings out new and old treasures from the storeroom" (CEV). One application of Jesus' teaching is the need to develop the ability to listen to other people. We have to go into the storeroom of our heart where we've stored the treasures of God's Word and pull out the principle and the passage that apply most appropriately to their current need.

Whenever God brings to mind that perfect verse or that key principle, you'll sense it. It just feels right. As Prov 25:11 states, "A word fitly spoken is like apples of gold in a setting of silver." We can trust that God will honor his Word and will use it to accomplish his work through us, as we're faithful in studying it and bold in applying it in our spiritual conversations. The Bible isn't like other books. It's alive and powerful (Heb 4:12). God has promised that he'll use his Word. We can bank on it. As God, by means of the prophet Isaiah, poetically declares, "For as the rain and the snow come down from heaven and do not return there but water the earth, making it bring forth and sprout, giving seed to the sower and bread to the eater, so shall my word be that goes out from my mouth; it shall not return to me empty, but it shall accomplish that which I purpose, and shall succeed in the thing for which I sent it" (Isa 55:10–11).

Assessing Receptivity and Responding Appropriately

Another factor we must take into account is the level of a person's receptivity. The underlying cause of someone's lack of receptivity may well be one of the aforementioned obstacles. No matter what the obstacles may be that keep people from coming to faith in Christ, each person with whom we speak has a different degree of receptivity both to us as individuals and to the message we're seeking to share with them.

Jimmy Scroggins and Steve Wright in *Turning Everyday Conversations into Gospel Conversations* classify responses to our attempts to inject spiritual subjects into everyday conversations as red-light, yellow-light, and green-light responses. Scroggins and Wright allude to the Apostle Paul's gospel presentation to a crowd of pagan listeners at the Areopagus in Athens. Paul's message elicits varied responses: first, the red-light response—"some mocked"; next, the yellow-light response—"others said, 'We will hear you again about this'"; and finally, the green-light response—"some men joined him and believed" (Acts 17:32–34). The underlying idea is that, even though we believe that everyone needs to hear about Jesus, and the need to present the gospel message to everyone is urgent, it's generally more effective to listen first and be sensitive to the respective level of receptivity of each person and proceed accordingly.[1]

Another important factor to bear in mind when determining how to best proceed in our spiritual conversations with others is the need to treat others ethically. Ethicists Tom Beauchamp and James Childress lay out four key principles in *Principles of Biomedical Ethics* that have been widely accepted in the field of medicine: *autonomy, nonmaleficence, beneficence,* and *justice.* These same principles are a helpful guide for those in other fields as well, including those of us who are seeking to help people with their spiritual health.[2]

- The principle of *autonomy* has to do with respecting the right of others to make decisions for themselves. It means that those we are seeking to serve shouldn't feel coerced or pressured to accept the service we're offering them. It implies that

1. Scroggins and Wright, *Turning Everyday Conversations into Gospel Conversations,* 94.

2. Beauchamp and Childress, *Principles of Biomedical Ethics.* The idea of applying the principles of biomedical ethics to spiritual care was inspired by the Spiritual Care Curriculum produced by the Neighborhood Christian Clinic, available online at https://www.thechristianclinic.org/spiritual-care-curriculum/.

people should be fully informed of the implications of what we're offering them before asking them to make a decision.

- The principle of *nonmaleficence* means that, inasmuch as possible, the service we provide for others shouldn't harm them in any way. Though in certain circumstances, in order to avoid a greater harm, it's necessary to expose a patient to a comparatively lesser risk or harm, whenever we choose to do so, we should always seek at the same time to minimize as much as possible the harm or risk involved.

- The principle of *beneficence* is the flipside of the principle of nonmaleficence. It's the idea that we should seek to do all the good that's within our power to do to those whom we are serving. We shouldn't only seek to shield them from harm, but we should also seek to lead them, by means of the services we offer them, to a better quality of life.

- Finally, the principle of *justice* is the idea that those we serve should receive a fair and equitable share of the benefits we offer and that no one should be discriminated against in the distribution of goods and services we're offering. Both the burdens and benefits of the services we're offering should be fairly distributed among members of every group in the society in which we live and serve.

Though these principles are generally applicable in any field of service, when applying them in the area of spiritual health as we engage in spiritual conversations, there are certain factors we must take into consideration.

With regard to the principle of *autonomy*, we must respect the freedom of others to either accept or reject the gospel message we're sharing with them. At the same time, though, we ought to be aware of the urgency of the situation. Their eternal destiny is at stake. Our desire to spare the person the tragedy of eternal torment, the pain inflicted by a lifestyle of sin, and separation from God will lead us to not be indifferent toward their response to our evangelistic efforts.

Various passages of Scripture commend an attitude of urgency in our evangelism. The prophet Isaiah urged his readers to "seek the Lord while he may be found; call upon him while he is near" (Isa 55:6). John the Baptist urged his hearers to "repent, for the kingdom of heaven is at hand" (Matt 3:2). Matthew 4:17 informs us that Jesus himself "began to preach, saying, 'Repent, for the kingdom of heaven is at hand,'" and in Luke 13:3 he told his hearers, "No, I tell you; but unless you repent, you will all likewise perish."

Though this is indeed the case, we must also remember the oft-quoted adage, "A man convinced against his will is of the same opinion still."[3] When sharing the gospel with others, we should be sensitive to their response and level of receptivity to what we're saying.

In *Sowing, Reaping, Keeping,* Laurence Singlehurst shares the example of a bridge that only supports one ton of weight and a truck with a five-ton load that needs to get to the other side. In order to get the five-ton load safely to the other side it will be necessary to do so incrementally, one ton at a time.[4]

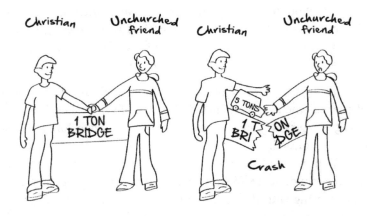

3. A version of this couplet appears in works such as Samuel Butler's 17th-century poem "Hudibras," and Mary Wollstonecraft's 1792 work, "A Vindication of the Rights of Woman," but is perhaps best known for its citation in Dale Carnegie's *How to Win Friends and Influence People.*

4. Singlehurst, *Sowing, Reaping, Keeping,* 29.

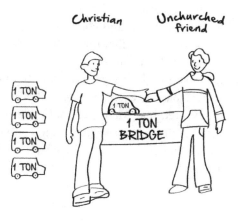

With regard to evangelism, it may be necessary to communicate the gospel little by little, in bite-size pieces that the person we're seeking to evangelize is able and willing to digest. This requires patience and insight in order to discern what elements of the gospel the person we're seeking to evangelize is prepared to hear and receive at the particular moment we're talking to them. Though the urgency of the situation might tempt us to try to get the whole five-ton load to the other side of the bridge in one crossing, our misguided attempts to do so too quickly may well destroy the bridge in the process and make it more difficult than ever to get the whole load safely to the other side.

As evangelists, we should also seek to abide by the principle of *nonmaleficence*. If we truly believe the Bible, we're conscious of the eternal harm inflicted by a person's choice to not accept the gospel. But at the same time, we're aware that manipulation and evangelistic methods that don't respect the principle of autonomy may cause psychological and spiritual harm to those we're seeking to rescue from hell. The balance can be delicate at times. A doctor may be aware that a patient's refusal to accept a certain line of treatment may end up causing him harm and at the same time be guided by her ethical responsibility to respect her patient's autonomy and freedom of choice regarding his decision to accept the recommended treatment. Because of this, we take care to explain well both the benefits and costs of what we're recommending. But we do so in a way that makes the person to whom we're talking feel respected and valued.

As we engage in spiritual conversations, we should also take into account the principle of *beneficence*. As believers in Christ, we're personally convinced that what we have to offer is of inestimable benefit to those with whom we're sharing. Yet we're aware that we live in a society in which people are constantly bombarded with the attempts of others to sell them something. Religious hucksters and charlatans use carefully devised strategies and techniques in order to convince others of their need for the product they're selling. As a result, it shouldn't surprise us when others are sometimes skeptical and standoffish with respect to our attempts to offer them the gift of salvation.

Knowing this, we must do everything within our power to tear down these walls of resistance by means of our sincerity, humility, and genuine friendship. As has often been said, the attitude we should adopt as evangelists is that of one beggar telling another beggar where to find food. Even though we believe that eternal salvation and a life of fellowship with God is the greatest good others may possibly obtain, the principle of beneficence should guide us to desire and do what we can to contribute to positive things in other aspects of their life. These aspects may be beyond their spiritual health, such as their economic wellbeing, physical health, healthy relationships, etc. If we're truly following the principle of beneficence, we do this not merely as a bait-and-switch strategy to get them to open up to the spiritual message we hope they'll receive, but because we're truly interested in their physical and social wellbeing as well.

Finally, as evangelists, we should also be guided by the principle of *justice*. This means we shouldn't allow any personal prejudice to keep us from sharing the good news of salvation, nor do it in such a way that precludes them from receiving the full benefit of the message we might offer to someone else with different characteristics. While it's important to be sensitive to the level of receptivity of the person to whom we're talking, we must not assume another person's level of openness or resistance to the gospel on the basis of their demographics. This may include someone's ethnicity, nationality, gender, or sexual orientation.

Jesus said he came to seek and to save the lost. While it's possible to discriminate against someone who's generally regarded as undesirable or inferior from one's own cultural perspective, it's also possible to be intimidated by those who may be viewed as privileged or powerful. While it's true that Jesus said it's harder for a rich man to enter the kingdom of heaven than for a camel to pass through the eye of a needle, we should remember that he also said immediately afterward that "with God all things are possible" (Matt 19:23–26). In other words, we should be careful to not write off anyone as being beyond the grasp of the gospel.

7

Christian Growth

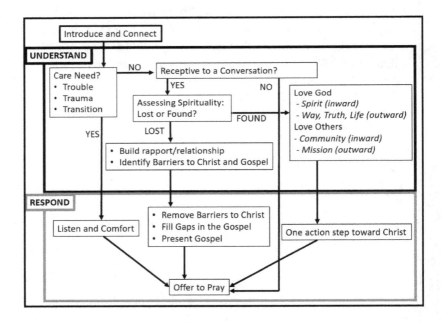

Do you ever feel like you're not growing in your relationship with Jesus? We've all felt that way many times. We want to grow but just feel stagnant. Why, though we desire growth, do we not feel like we're growing? We pray, but maybe we need to pray more. We read the Bible, but maybe we need to read the Bible more. But somewhere in our heart we sense that neither of those is the answer. It's not that the Bible and prayer are unimportant. They are essential to growth in a relationship with Jesus. However, when we have a healthy amount of those things, we may need more if we're going to grow as Jesus desires us to grow.

The primary vision of spiritual growth we're given in Scripture is a fruit-bearing plant (John 15:1–9). A healthy, fruit-bearing plant has a source of nourishment. It not only grows, but it reproduces and bears fruit. Jesus said, "I am the vine, you are the branches. Whoever abides in me and I in him, he it is that bears much fruit, for apart from me you can do nothing" (John 15:5). You can't be healthy spiritually apart from living in connection to Christ.

Growth isn't something you can control. A plant can't grow of its own will. Unlike a plant, however, God has given us proactive means to influence our growth. I'm reminded of Psalm 1, where we're promised that if we avoid the ways characterized by certain types of people (the wicked, sinners, mockers), and instead delight in the law of the Lord, we will be just like a tree that has all it needs to grow and bear fruit.

What, then, is spiritual growth? *Spiritual growth happens when a person's whole life is nourished by Christ's love and bears Christ's fruit of love toward others.*

As you place yourself where you can be nourished by Christ, growth happens. To go back to where we've been, we said in chapter 3 that God reveals *four places* in Scripture where you can reliably find him. This means you must choose to be with him in those places if you want to grow in Christ. Each of these four places is intimately related to what Jesus said are *the greatest commandments*: to love God and love others.

So spiritual growth will always have to do with cultivating your love for God and for others.

- Love God
  - Inward: *spirit*
  - Outward: *way, truth, life*
- Love Others
  - Inward: *community of faith*
  - Outward: *mission*

Each of these aspects of spiritual growth has an inward and an outward expression. Inwardly, there's a way our identity is formed by love for God and love for others. That same love is expressed outwardly as we choose to live in ways that are consistent with who we are in Christ. In our spiritual conversations, if we want to help the person grow in Christ, we want to ask some questions in these four areas. This will give us a clue where God may want to help them grow. In this chapter, we'll look at these four areas and how we grow in each, as well as consider some diagnostic questions we might ask to assess how a person is doing in each area.

Spirit—The Inward Aspect of Loving God

When I (Jim) was a youth pastor, I would often hear a student say something like this: "If I lived when Jesus was alive in the flesh, it would be so much easier to believe in him." The idea is that it's easier to connect with a physical being than it is with a metaphysical God. But nothing could be further from the truth! Because God isn't restricted by location, we can have twenty-four-hour, seven-day-a-week access to him. Further, God can speak directly to my soul without the use of words. I could never have that close of a relationship with another human being. If we want to love or connect with Jesus, one foundational way that we connect with him is in our *spirit*. In John 4:24, Jesus says that anyone who wants to worship God must worship him in spirit and in truth. Our spirit is the part of us that loves God at a personal, individual level. We give and receive love from God inwardly in our spirit.

But just because we can have access to God does not necessarily mean we take advantage of that relationship. The two primary ways we cultivate our love for God in our spirit are through right beliefs (orthodoxy) and right practices (orthopraxy). In other words, we need to believe the right things about God, ourselves, and the world. And we need to have the best means by which we engage our personal relationship with God. A personal relationship with God requires both.

Think of what it would be like to have a relationship that's missing one of these things. The closest personal relationship I (Jim) have, outside of with God, is with my wife. Imagine if I described all the practices we use to engage our relationship. I take her on dates. I write her love notes. I buy her gifts. I actually talk to her over meals instead of looking at my phone (so romantic, I know). As an outsider looking in, you would say I have a great relationship with my wife. But what if I told you that I do all those things because I believe she'll punish me if I don't? That wouldn't be a love relationship, would it? Of course not! Yet, many Christians have a "quiet time" (prayer and Bible study), go to church, and even tithe out of a fear that if they don't, God will curse them in some way. I've heard in church that if I don't have a quiet time, God won't bless my day. That's not a love relationship. That's not the way God loves us, nor is it a good way to love him. Does God want me to read my Bible and pray? Yes! He wants me to do those things out of a desire to love him and know him more. It isn't about having all the right practices, but allowing those practices to be a means by which we love God.

Well, if that's the case, can we just have a love for God absent of practices? Think about it this way: What's the difference between a stalker and a lover? Both have all the same information. They both know what their object of affection is wearing today, what car they drive, and where they are right now. Both know all the intimate details of that person's life. The difference between a stalker and a lover isn't the information, but an actual interaction with that person. A relationship of love requires interaction. As Christians, we can have all the right beliefs, truths, and information about God—and that would be a good thing—but if we don't have actual practices whereby we interact with God, then we may just be stalkers. We need beliefs and practices to cultivate our love for God.

This may sound ridiculous, but we may be guilty of reciting Bible verses, knowing the right theological answers, and even singing worship songs without drawing near to God. The presence of right beliefs or biblical truth does not ensure that we love God. Beliefs and practices are the means by which we grow or cultivate our love for God. But the end is love for God. When we try to make the goal having a quiet time, or knowing the answers, we soon get off track. So how can we love God through our spirit? So, what are the beliefs and practices that will help us in our walk with God?

Orthodoxy—Right Beliefs

In order to cultivate a love relationship with God, we need to think and believe right things. This is not just about theology or doctrine, but about everything. Or to be more accurate, our theology and doctrine impact how we think and believe about everything. We like to think of our religious beliefs as being separate, but theology is foundational to everything else we think or believe about ourselves, other people, and the world we inhabit. God created all things, therefore what he says things are like is true. And because he created all things, everything in our lives has its source in him. There is no way to separate God from our lives. Your life is an integrated whole under God's lordship, whether you acknowledge it or not. In order to live well, we must align our beliefs about reality with what God says is actually true.

Herein lies the trouble. How do we know if we have the right beliefs? There are so many denominations because there are many perspectives on what beliefs are right and which are, well, heretical. While this isn't the place to work through those differences, there are some things we as Christians should be able to agree on. For example, one of the oldest and most widely accepted statements of belief can be found in the Apostle's Creed:

> I believe in God, the Father almighty,
>
> creator of heaven and earth.
>
> I believe in Jesus Christ, his only Son, our Lord.
>
> He was conceived by the power of the Holy Spirit
>
> and born of the virgin Mary.
>
> He suffered under Pontius Pilate,
>
> was crucified, died, and was buried.

He descended to the dead.

On the third day he rose again.

He ascended into heaven,

and is seated at the right hand of the Father.

He will come again to judge the living and the dead.

I believe in the Holy Spirit,

the holy catholic Church,

the communion of the saints,

the forgiveness of sins,

the resurrection of the body,

and the life everlasting. Amen.

It's important to note, though, that any creed is only good to the degree it's supported by the Bible. We should also have a robust belief or acceptance that the Bible is God's Word and therefore authoritative.

Further, what we *say* we believe may be different than what we *actually* believe. To put it another way, how we live is a better indicator of what we actually believe than what we say we believe. For example, we may say that we believe that all people are created in the image of God and worthy of respect. But how we treat that guy who just cut us off in traffic will demonstrate the extent to which we actually believe that.

Belief is not as cut and dry as we'd like it to be. Many Christians speak of their belief system as if it were a simple case of "either you do or you don't." In reality, beliefs are graded, meaning we can more or less believe something. Here's what we mean. Think about a grade in a class. You can pass a class with an A or a D, but you still pass. Though you pass, there is a difference in the quality of passing. We may 60 percent believe that God is good. On a good day, we recognize God's goodness—and we're right to do so—but when tragedy strikes, we may be tempted to think God isn't as good as we thought he was. God's goodness hasn't changed, but the level in which we trust in his goodness has.

Further, the "grade" with which we believe something changes for better or worse over time. God may use our experiences and the experiences of others to increase our belief that God is good. This happens when we hear the testimony of a faithful person who experienced the same tragedy we did and God met them in a tangible way. Though we didn't experience it ourselves, we can lean on their experience to help us grow.

God is very gracious to us in that he doesn't require us to have all the right beliefs nor the highest "grade" of belief in order to have a relationship with him. He lovingly invites us to a relationship and then begins his good work of shaping and forming our beliefs over time. The goal is not to have all the right beliefs, but to love God. But it takes practice to help us grow that relationship.

Orthopraxy—Right Practices

In addition to right beliefs, we need right practices to grow in our love for God. Practices are those habits, disciplines, or activities that cultivate our relationship with God. Some of these are intentional. In many Christian circles, these are called spiritual disciplines.

There are a few practices that are essential. For example, it would be impossible to have a relationship with God without a practice of prayer. Prayer can be defined simply as talking to God. We must talk to God to have a relationship with him. Many of us struggle with prayer because we think we have to be in a particular state of mind or even a special place to pray. There may well be some value to that, but we can also pray anytime, anywhere, about anything. Paul tells us to "pray without ceasing" (1 Thess 5:17). God desires for us to draw near to him in all circumstances.

Prayer isn't just about talking, but also about listening. We've all been in conversations where the other person did all the talking. It's not much of a relationship. We get the sense that person could have just as easily been talking to a brick wall. In prayer, we also want to listen. One great way to listen to God is to read his Word, the Bible. He's already spoken to us through his Word. It's living, active, and able to go beyond the surface and speak right to our heart (Heb 4:12). As we study and understand God's Word, he uses it as a way of speaking to us.

There's great value in memorizing Scripture. It's like learning the language of God. If you had a friend who spoke only Spanish, your relationship with them would be difficult to cultivate because of the language barrier. You could find ways of communicating through sounds, gestures, and visual cues. But if you learned Spanish, it would significantly open up your ability to communicate. As you memorize Scripture, God can bring that verse or phrase to your heart in the moment you need it. You may not have your Bible handy or know where to find it if you don't have it memorized.

Another way of listening to God is to actually, well, listen. God can speak to your heart directly through his Holy Spirit. Hearing from God is much more about relationally connecting with him than it is about hearing a specific word or message. God may tell you to do something or even give you some secret revelation, but to approach God with that expectation puts an unhealthy pressure on your relationship with God. Psalm 46:10 encourages us to "be still and know that (he) is God." There's good in just being in his presence and acknowledging who he is without expecting anything more. If God does speak to you in some specific way, though, you can have confidence that it will never violate his Word. It's a very good practice to bring what you hear from God before other mature Christians before acting on it. The important thing to note here, though, is that a relationship with God requires both speaking and listening.

While prayer and Bible reading are foundational practices we must have in order to cultivate a relationship with God, there are many more practices that are also helpful. These include fasting, solitude, service, confession, celebration, worship, reflection, simplicity, and thankfulness. Some find great value in things like going on a nature walk or reading Christian authors. Remember that the goal is not having all the right beliefs or all the right practices. The ultimate goal is a sincere love for God. There are people who may have all the right beliefs and practices yet be far from the love of God (Matt 7:21–23). This was the case with the Pharisees (Matt 15:8–9) and could also be the case with us if our focus is not on the love of God.

There are some habits or disciplines that are somewhat unintentional. For example, if you wake up in the morning and the first thing you do every day is check your social media, that influences you. We're not commenting on the rightness or wrongness of that habit. But checking social media instead of, say, taking a minute to pray and thank God for another day will form you in some way. What you do on your commute to work influences you. How often you pick up your phone to check for notifications has an impact on you. It's good for us to think through these things and how they shape our soul or spirit.

Diagnostic Questions about Spirit

When we're having a spiritual conversation with someone whom we know is a Christian, this is one key area where we can ask questions. We want to learn more about their beliefs and practices to see how we might help them take a step toward Jesus. We'll ask them questions about these areas. As you ask questions, remember that the goal is to listen and understand the person and help shepherd them toward identifying one step they would like to take toward Jesus. Once you've identified that step, there's no need to continue.

What diagnostic questions might you ask someone to determine where they're at spiritually? At each step, we'll offer a few that have been helpful for us (and that we've used tens of thousands of times).

- *What spiritual practices do you regularly use to grow or maintain your faith?*

This question helps you determine what the person's already doing. You may ask some follow-up questions to see how consistent they are in the practice. For example, you might say, "You said you read your Bible. What does that look like for you?" You're not looking for a minimum amount. You're just trying to understand. If the person says five minutes a day, that may not sound like much to you, but it may be a huge step of faith for them. We're not judging what the person is doing, but learning. You might ask, "What have you learned?" Or maybe, "How has that practice been for you?"

While most people might feel they ought to add a practice or action, there are some who need to give themselves a break. There are some who have good practices that are motivated by a desire to earn God's love. As Dallas Willard said, "Grace is not opposed to effort, it is opposed to earning. Earning is an attitude. Effort is an action."[1] These actions may be good; but the heart is not that of love, but of earning.

Behind our practices are beliefs that fuel or motivate our actions. We must assess the person's beliefs. *Why* questions will help us here. It can be difficult to identify our true *why*. Many of us will offer the answers that we think we ought to say rather than what is our true motivation. There is some value in stating true things even when our heart isn't fully there; but in order to have the greatest growth, we also need to honestly examine our hearts. You may learn to ask deeper *why* questions and even gently and lovingly push the person to help them name their motivation. Remember that the goal is to help the person identify an *action* step. This may be less about adding a practice and more about taking time to examine their own hearts.

Another question you can ask to identify an action step might be this: *Which spiritual practices do you wish you used more?* The goal of this question is to help identify what practices the person would like to engage in to grow. Many people fail to take an action step because they don't have a good goal. We need to help people develop a good goal. A good way to do this is to use "S.M.A.R.T. Goals."[2]

A SMART goal is:

1. Willard, *The Great Omission*, 61, 80.

2. Doran et al., "There's a S.M.A.R.T. Way to Write Management's Goals and Objectives," 70.

- Specific—Here you want to get as clear as you can.

- Measurable—In other words, I know how I am tracking on my goal and if I achieved it or not.

- Attainable—It's realistic for you to actually do it.

- Relevant—It's worth your time and energy and means something to you.

- Time-bound—There's a deadline. You know whether or not you achieved it and there is an end date.

Why are SMART goals important? Let's say someone told you, "I'd like to lose weight." Is that a good goal? What does it even mean? Do I want to lose one pound or twenty pounds? And, by when? Wanting to lose weight is a good thing, but not a good goal. If I say I want to lose twenty pounds in six months so I can get off my blood pressure medications, that's a good goal! While this seems obvious, sometimes people say, "I want to pray more," or, "I want to read the Bible more." Often that good desire is not matched with a good goal.

I (Jim) remember when my friend Brad came to me and said, "I really want to pray more." I asked him what was holding him back. He said he had a landscaping business that required him to work from sunup to sundown and was so tired when he got home he didn't have time to do anything but eat, shower, and get ready for the next day.

I asked, "What do you do when you're on the lawnmower?"

He said, "I usually listen to music." I asked, "What if just on the first yard of the day, you pray? Do you think you could try that three times this week?" Brad said, "Sure!"

This is how a SMART goal works. I just helped him develop a SMART goal. He had one week to pray three times on his first lawn of the day. By the end of that week, he'd know whether he'd done it or not. I could ask him questions to see how it went. If it went well, I could celebrate with him. If it didn't go well, I could help him set a new goal based on the experience. Either way, it was a step toward Jesus Christ.

About two weeks later, Brad came back to me and said, "You won't believe what happened! I did what you said—and man, I don't know what happened, but I was praying, and God's peace just flooded me. I had to be smiling like an idiot on that mower!" I got to celebrate with Brad!

Here's the deal: I didn't do that. God did! Brad took the very simple step of faith of trusting God by trying a SMART goal, and God met him on a mower. We never know how God might respond, but we always want to take a step toward Jesus out of a sincere desire to love him. SMART goals will help us in every aspect of life. As you read through these four areas, remember that you can always use the SMART-goal tool.

Now many Christians stop here at "Spirit" in describing what it means to have a relationship with God. While loving God through a personal relationship "in spirit" is the most foundational and essential element of our faith, there's more to life and our walk with God than this.

Way, Truth, Life—The Outward Aspect of Loving God

The book of John is different from the other Gospels. John is writing to the Greeks, whereas Matthew, Mark, and Luke are writing to the Jews. Accordingly, John expresses Jesus' identity in ways that would be understandable to Greeks. In John 1:1 he calls Jesus the "word" (using the Greek word *logos*). This word *logos* had a rich history among Greeks. It had been used by Greek philosophers for centuries to describe a unifying principle that would hold the universe together. When John called Jesus *logos*, he was saying to the Greeks, "The *logos* you are seeking is not a principle or idea, but a person who is God!" Imagine how earth-shattering that would have been.

Now imagine how John 14:6 was received by the Greek listener: "Jesus said to him, 'I am the way, and the truth, and the life. No one comes to the Father except through me.'" Jesus didn't merely claim to *know* the way, truth, and life. Jesus didn't merely claim to be able to *show* the way, truth, and life. Jesus said he *is* the way, truth, and life. As you align yourself with God's way, God's truth, and God's design for life, you're aligning yourself with Jesus himself. If you want to be where Jesus is, you must live according to his way, his truth, and his life.

What does it mean to live according to God's way, truth, and life? This is largely about the outward choices we make in life. In Christian circles, we often talk about how we *steward* our life. Certainly, this flows from our "spirit," or the beliefs and practices we talked about earlier, but it's important for us to examine this aspect of our outward lives. As we seek to live according to God's ways, we need to think about two categories: *ethics* and *essences*.

Ethics

Ethics are those moral principles that guide our choices. We make decisions based on what we view as right and wrong, good and evil, or even just good, better, and best. The choices we make are informed by our understanding of what's good and right. For Christians, God prescribes certain things to do and other things to avoid. For example, we should exhibit the fruit of the Spirit in our lives (Gal 5:22). We should be compassionate, kind, patient, humble, and gentle (Col 3:12). We should be generous (2 Cor 9:6–8), particularly to the poor (Prov 19:17). There are also certain things the Bible tells us to avoid. We should avoid lying, stealing, idolatry, infidelity, murder, and coveting (Exod 20:1–17). We should avoid gossip and slander (Jas 4:11). There are many prescriptive, ethical standards that God has revealed to us in his Word to help us live well in this world. As we live according to these standards, we have an opportunity to connect with God.

Most of the time, when we discuss "Way, Truth, Life" in church, it's framed only in terms of ethics. However, considering ethical categories alone isn't enough. There's more we need to consider in order to live according to God's ways, truth, and life.

Essences

Essences refers to the way things are. This is about discovering God's truth by understanding his design. God also reveals his ways through how he made things, which may or may not be described in the Bible, and may or may not fit our ethical categories. Take gravity, for example. Let's say someone tells you, "I don't believe gravity is real. I can't find a Bible verse about it. I'm going to climb up on my roof and jump off." They're perfectly free to do that. Would they be violating an ethical standard? Not necessarily. Is there a Bible verse we can show them to get them to stop? Nope. But there are consequences for that decision. They may end up with a broken limb or worse. Gravity is *the way things are*. They may not be able to find it in the Bible, but that doesn't mean that God doesn't care about how they act with respect to gravity. He does care, and one of the ways they can live in accordance with his reality is to respect the way he made things.

That example seems absurd, but think of some other ways we might violate God's design. If someone doesn't maintain a healthy weight and diet, they'll have long-term health issues. You may not be able to find a Bible verse about it, and you may not consider it an ethical issue; but it matters to God, and he's shown there are better and worse ways of living through the way he made our bodies. The book of Proverbs is largely about this category. Proverbs is a collection of wisdom sayings. Many proverbs were gleaned from life, while others were outright plagiarized from other wisdom sources. This claim may cause the scholar's hackles to go up, but citing your sources was not an Ancient Near Eastern practice. The ancients were more concerned about getting the truth of a statement across, regardless of where they got that statement from. Proverbs reveals that there are ways of going about your job, your finances, your health, your relationships, and so on. We may not put these into ethical categories, but nonetheless God has revealed his truth through the way he designed this world.

Diagnostic Questions about Way, Truth, Life

When having a spiritual conversation with someone we know is a Christian, here is another key area where we can ask questions. We want to learn more about the outward choices they make and how they align with God's ways, truth, and life. We want to understand not only ethical and moral aspects of their life, but how they can better steward their life unto God. Remember, the goal is not to live the perfect ethical life, or the best, healthy life in every area. That is certainly good, and we'd love to see that for anyone. Instead, the goal is to love God and serve him through the life we live on this earth. As you ask questions, remember that the goal is to listen and understand the person and help shepherd them toward identifying one step they'd like to take toward Jesus. Once you've identified that step, there's no need to continue.

What diagnostic questions might you ask someone to determine where they are in respect to living according to God's way, truth, and life? These types of questions tend to come up very naturally, but we don't label them as spiritual. When someone's talking about the "normal" spaces of their life, we can begin to think about spiritual questions we might ask. For example, in our interactions with patients, some will indicate difficulty losing weight or complying with their medicines. There are very practical questions the medical provider may ask, but we may also ask, "Have you ever prayed and asked God to help you?" This isn't meant to evoke guilt, but to encourage the person to integrate their faith in every aspect of their life. They've already told us that they're a Christian, so we want to help them grow through these diagnostic questions.

If someone shares a struggle with finances or finding a job, we might ask, "What would you ask God to do for you if he asked you right now?" This gets them thinking about God's role in their life and also gives us a clear way to pray with and for them.

If the person shares with us how they're living immorally, we want to not only receive them with compassion and lack of judgment, but also challenge them to consider God's ways. Perhaps they don't know any better. Or maybe they've never considered an alternative way. We don't want to assume disobedience on their part. Instead, we can lovingly and gently show them God's Word and encourage them to take that issue to him.

One potentially delicate area of dealing with people in this area is the need to confront people with their sinful behavior and steer them toward behavioral change. In the discipleship process, the occasion inevitably arises when we must confront others with sinful habits and behavior in their life. This is a sensitive issue on which a lot of wisdom and tact is needed. Ideally, in the case of professing believers, a local church should be involved in the process of confronting others with their sin and seeking to steer them toward repentance and restoration. But there will be occasions in which we as fellow believers will have the opportunity to call others to repentance and a lifestyle of greater holiness. In general, we need to win the right to speak into someone's life on these types of issues that only comes by way of mutual trust and relationship.

Whatever the issue might be, the goal is to help the person think about their ways and how those align with God's way. Many times this is clear from Scripture, and other times it takes more reflecting on how what God has revealed leads to human flourishing. Regardless, our goal is to love God with our lives and honor him with the choices we make. This is always best done in community.

Community of Faith—The Inward Aspect of Loving Others

You might think of the community of faith as "the church," but often our church is not a true community of faith. I (Jim) did not grow up in the South, but one thing that surprised me upon moving here was discovering that upon first meeting, people will ask you, "Where do you go to church?" The effect in a culture where everyone is asked that question is that everyone has an answer, regardless of whether they really go to church or not. To grow in our love for God and our love for others, we must have more than an answer to the "Where do you go to church?" question. We need a community of faith.

A community of faith is a group of Christians with whom we share life and love. They know us, and we know them. They love us, and we love them. What unites us is our shared love for Jesus and finding our fundamental identity as being his followers. If we're going to love God and love people, we must be in a community of faith. In John 15:9–17, Jesus intimately ties our love for him with our love for others, culminating in the command to love one another. The first Epistle of John is largely about how our love for God and for fellow believers is woven together. Among the clearest expressions of this relationship is where John ends by saying, "whoever loves God must also love his brother" (1 John 4:7–21). This is about interacting with Jesus. In Matt 18:20, Jesus tells us that where two or more are gathered in his name, he's present with them. If we want to love Jesus, we must love other Christians.

What does this Christian community look like? The picture we get in Acts 2 is that of giving and receiving. They gathered together and "had all things in common" (Acts 2:44–45). They shared their time, talents, possessions, and lives. Let's talk about giving and receiving.

Giving

Giving means that we give of ourselves, not just receive. This isn't just about finances (though that's included). It's about love for others. Are we opening ourselves up to people? Are we sharing with others? Many today have chided "consumer Christians" who just go to church to get something. They're not interested in giving, but only in getting something out of the worship service. That's certainly a selfish orientation toward the church and isn't love for others. To love, we must be willing to give. Jesus defined love in John 15 as giving up ourselves for others. If we want to be in community with others, we must give of ourselves.

Receiving

In order to have community, we must also receive from others. Receiving means we welcome others in the community to love, serve, and bless us. While we all know that the consumer Christian is selfish, many of us are willing to give but don't want to receive. As pastors, we know this temptation. We're willing to give sermons, do hospital visits, direct resources to those in need, or listen patiently in a pastoral counseling session. But we'd never share our hurts or grief with those that we served as a pastor. That's pride, and it keeps us from being in true community with others. That is like Peter refusing to have his feet washed by Jesus. Jesus' response was, "If I do not wash you, you have no share with me" (John 13:8). There's something about receiving that helps us belong.

Again, though, the goal isn't to outdo others in giving or receiving. The goal isn't to give and receive in all the right ways. As good as those goals might be, the goal is love for others out of love for God. We gather, give, receive, and worship God together out of mutual love, which is community.

Diagnostic Questions about Community

When we're having a spiritual conversation with someone we know is a Christian, community is another key area where we can ask questions. We want to learn more about their community of faith. We want to understand not only the frequency with which they attend church, but just how supported they are by their church. Do they give of themselves to a group of people? As you ask questions, remember that the goal is to listen, understand the person, and help shepherd them toward identifying one step they would like to take toward Jesus. Once you've identified that step, there's no need to continue.

What diagnostic questions might you ask someone to determine how rooted they are in a community of faith? Asking people some simple questions to start is key. You might ask them, "Do you have a church home?" If the answer is yes, you might be able to discern some things by how they respond, without asking more questions. Or you might say, "Tell me about the ways you're involved there." Knowing how often someone attends could be helpful as well. But as you might guess, going to church doesn't guarantee that someone has community.

One question that we find really helps orient us is this: *If something significant were to happen in your life (such as a house fire or cancer diagnosis), who are the people who'd come alongside you to both encourage you in your faith and pray for you, as well as provide your practical needs?* —and it must be both.

How the person answers that question will help us determine if they have a true community of faith. Think of your own answer. If you say, "Well, I don't have anyone who'd do both," that means you don't have a community of faith. Maybe you'd say, "That wouldn't be my church; that would be my family." Then your family is effectively your community of faith. There's no need to feel guilty if that's your answer. But God's desire for us is to have community in Christ. It's one of the ways that we can grow in our love for others, but also with God himself. He's present in our gatherings. And we think it's healthy to find that community not just with our family, but with a diverse group of people beyond our family that covenant together to live as a New Testament church.

Proverbs 17:17 tells us, "A friend loves at all times, and a brother [or sister] is born for a time of adversity" (NIV). You don't realize how much you need community until times of adversity hit, such as a house fire or cancer diagnosis. Here's the problem, though. You have to invest in developing community before the storms of life hit. It takes time to build community. People don't become friends overnight. You don't consider someone you just met a true brother or sister. We must invest in community before those times of adversity come. Then you'll have love and support in the midst of difficult times. You can also be the support for others in their difficult times. The goal, though, is to love at all times.

Mission—The Outward Aspect of Loving Others

In church circles there's an unspoken tension about what the primary mission of the Body of Christ should be. On one hand, you have *social gospel* churches that believe that Jesus' mission is all about meeting the tangible needs of people. You might even hear *social gospel* churches misquoting St. Francis of Assisi, "Preach the gospel at all times—and if necessary, use words." The idea is that Christians should preach with their lives and actions primarily, and their words secondarily, if at all.

On the other hand, you have *spoken gospel* churches that believe Jesus' mission is all about bringing people to salvation in Jesus Christ. As a youth pastor, I (Jim) served at a church that sent a group of teens to do international missionary work among a very poor community of refugees. Year after year, this little suburban church would spend tens of thousands of dollars and send dozens of teenagers down to present the plan of salvation to VBS-saturated refugees who were greeted each summer by ten other youth groups like ours. One summer, I suggested we go down to the poor community to listen to these refugees and see if there were any tangible needs we could meet. When I talked to the missionary about this idea, he looked me in the eye and said, "Jim, we just need to give them the gospel." Underlying his statement was a theology that says that meeting the actual, tangible needs of people is less important than preaching the gospel. Meeting needs, in this missionary's mind, was not *gospel* work.

In many ways this is why we started this book explaining the "big gospel." The tension like the one between a *social gospel* and a *spoken gospel* unnecessarily creates a mutual exclusion in which one of the two isn't necessary. It truncates one aspect of Christ's mission in favor of another. The reality is that God's mission includes both serving others in the name of Christ and sharing with others the name of Christ. This is the outward expression of our love for others. We love others by serving them. But this isn't just about loving others, but also about loving God. If you want to be close to Jesus, you must be focused on his mission as well.

Think of this: God ties his presence to his mission. On the heels of the Great Commission, Jesus says, "And behold, I am with you always, even to the end of the age" (Matt 28:20). In Acts 1:8, when Jesus told his disciples they'd be his witnesses, it was in the wake of the promise of the Holy Spirit, which is God's presence with them. In Matt 25:40, when Jesus spoke of the ways his disciples would tangibly meet the needs of others, he said it would be done directly to and for him. If you want to be close to Jesus, you must both serve and share.

Serving

Christ's mission includes meeting the specific tangible needs in someone's life. The way we do this can be quite varied, depending on what the person's needs are. It could be raking leaves for a disabled neighbor. It could be babysitting so a married couple with small children can spend some time investing in their marriage. It can be working at a soup kitchen, binding wounds, giving water out on a hot day, or simply listening.

There are times when a person's needs are not spoken or obvious. Many assume that every homeless person is looking for a handout. And some may be asking for money. But what many of the homeless people we know really want is dignity and respect. Imagine if everyone you passed avoided you and tried not to make eye contact with you. It would take a toll on you. Perhaps the most important need you could meet is just to talk and listen.

Another way we serve others is by being involved in our communities and neighborhoods and seeking to promote *shalom* through whatever practical means we have available. Generally, this means taking the time to listen to others, build relationships, and empower those who may need some extra encouragement and practical assistance in their lives to be the leaders God has called them to be.

Sharing

Christ's mission is also about sharing. There's a message to be proclaimed. This isn't just about bringing people to salvation, but about seeing every person move closer to Jesus. What you're learning in this book is about sharing Christ with others. Whether the person you talk to is a Christian or not, it's Christ's mission to make disciples through sharing his words.

One mistake Christians often make is to think that this task is only the function of one's local church. While sharing with others through discipleship and evangelism is best done in participation with a local church, all of us are called to share. The church and its leaders are to equip you for ministry (Eph 4:12). That ministry oftentimes should happen beyond the walls of the church. It may not be part of your *job* to share with others, but as followers of Jesus we want to be about his mission.

The Mission Is Love

There are some Christians who seem to do everything right. You might picture Ned Flanders from The Simpsons. They go to church every time the doors are open. They read their Bible and pray every day. They live a flawless moral life and seem to do everything God requires. These gold-medal Christians are winning the religiosity competition in the spiritual Olympics. Yet there are some of these "super Christians" who come across as judgmental or holier-than-thou. Accompanying this pious mindset may be pride.

Jesus had quite a bit to say to the most religious people of his time (perhaps the most scathing bit is from Matt 23). The Apostle Paul made it clear that our outward choices do not matter if they aren't done out of love (1 Cor 13:1–3). Often the outward indicator of our inward love for others is what we're calling *mission* in this book. But we want to be clear that *mission* isn't ultimately about doing everything right, or trying to win spiritual contests, but about love and serving others.

I (Jim) remember walking through downtown Chicago one day and coming across a man with a bullhorn proclaiming what he believed to be the gospel. His version was harsh and emphasized the fires of hell significantly more than the grace of Jesus Christ. Curious, I stopped to ask him this question: "How many people stop and respond to your message?"

"Not very many," he replied. My suspicion was no one.

So, I asked, "Then why do you do it?"

Before I tell you his answer, I believe there is value in proclaiming a message even if no one responds (Isa 6:9–10). But if there isn't a response, I also think it warrants asking why.

His response was this: "I don't care if they respond. My job is to proclaim so they'll have no excuse."

What struck me was how unloving that was. Jesus told us that the greatest commandments are about love. Of course, we need to care whether people respond or not! Of course, we need to tweak our approach in ways that help us love more effectively! We should still be faithful even if people don't respond, but that doesn't give us an excuse to be selfish in the mission. Yet in some strange way, God even uses selfish proclamations of his gospel (Phil 1:15–18).

Diagnostic Questions about Mission

When we're having a spiritual conversation with someone we know is a Christian, mission is another key area about which we can ask questions. We want to learn more about how they reach out to others in love. We want to understand how they serve the tangible needs of others, particularly beyond the walls of the church. We might say something like, "Tell me about a time you met practical needs of people as an act of service to God." Then we can follow up with curiosity, seeking to understand the person on their own terms. We might want to ask about frequency and/or how long it's been since they've met someone's practical needs. Again, we're not seeking to judge, but to understand.

We also want to understand in what ways they share Christ's words with others through evangelism and discipleship. We might suggest, "Tell me about a time that you shared a Bible verse or a biblical message with someone." We could ask, "Do you have any people in your life in whom you're investing spiritually?" Remember, the goal is not to live the mission perfectly. That's certainly good, and we'd love to see that for anyone. But the goal is to love God and honor his mission by loving others.

The essence of what we're looking for is this: How much are we aligning our time and resources to God's agenda, rather than asking him to bless our agenda? Certainly, we have freedom to live life, but God has called us to be about his mission.

What diagnostic questions might you ask someone to determine where they are with respect to living out Christ's mission? The questions we ask aren't as important as intentionally engaging people about their spiritual lives and seeking to understand them on their own terms. Trust and acceptance are the soil in which spiritual conversations thrive. Some people take time to trust you. Others will trust you from the start. Regardless, we need to do our part to be people worthy of trust and who genuinely show interest in others. We're not imposing our agenda on people, but simply sensing where God is at work and partnering with him in the good work of seeing this person take a step toward Jesus Christ.

8

From Theory to Practice

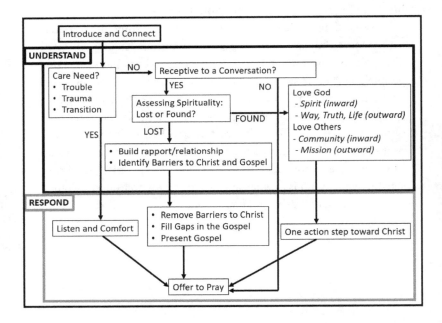

WE'VE HAD TENS OF thousands of conversations as part of the spiritual health ministry at Christ Community Health Services in Memphis, Tennessee. Though we'll share with you a set of go-to tools we typically use in our conversations with others, we want to emphasize that there's no set script. Each situation is unique. Each person with whom we engage in a spiritual conversation brings their own unique set of circumstances to the table, and we must take this into account. Nevertheless, we've found that having a set of prepared questions, illustrations, and practical pointers helps to facilitate the conversation. These tools make conversations more productive. Let me (David) share with you what one of these visits with a patient might look like. Though your personal context may be very different than ours, our hope is that from this you'll be able to see aspects that can be used in your own spiritual conversations.

Breaking the Ice

First of all, it's important to introduce yourself and to inform the person of the purpose of the visit. This helps to ease tensions and prepare them. I typically say something like this: "Good morning! I'm David, the Spiritual Health Advisor here at Christ Community, and what I do is come in for a few minutes before the doctor in order to check up a bit on your spiritual health, listen, and encourage you in your spiritual life. I don't solve problems. But I would love to pray for you and ask God to help you today— if that's okay with you."

It's important at the very beginning to let the person know that we respect their right to refuse to talk about spiritual matters if they so choose. In our experience at Christ Community, roughly 3 percent of patients opt out of these conversations or say they prefer that we not pray for them. Whenever this happens, we just say something like the following: "No problem at all! The doctor will be in to see you soon. Have a great day!" We understand that for the majority of our patients the reason they're there is to see the doctor, not the Spiritual Health Advisor, and we want to communicate to them that we respect their time, privacy, and personal preferences.

Hopefully, the way we respond will open the door for someone else who may one day come behind us when they're more open to speak about these matters. On several occasions, we've had the chance to engage a patient who at first opted out of a spiritual health visit but on a future visit agreed to what turned out to be a fruitful conversation. This is a situation in which we need the guidance of the Lord. But in our opinion, it's best to err on the side of caution.

While I'm introducing myself, I often throw in the line, "I don't solve problems," as a touch of humor to break the ice. But at this moment I'm also communicating an important truth, which is that, ultimately, I'm not any better than they are. We're all on an equal footing before the Lord. I'm just a fellow pilgrim in the journey of life to share some encouragement and to lead them to the true source of help and healing in their life, God.

It's also important to be up front about our intentions for the conversation. We're not engaged in some sort of bait-and-switch sales technique. It's important that the person with whom we're talking sees us as trustworthy and honest.

During the introduction, I make a special point to pay attention to any non-verbal or verbal cues the person may give regarding their level of interest in the conversation. This helps me know how to proceed most effectively. Some people may be very interested in spiritual matters and communicate in one way or another that they are receptive. Others may be a bit more timid or unsure with regard to discussing these spiritual matters. It's important to smile and look at people at eye level in order to communicate empathy.

In any case, it's good to ask a few questions at the beginning of a conversation to demonstrate a personal interest in the person with whom we're talking: "How have things been going for you lately?" "Are you working somewhere?" "Tell me a bit about your family." "Do you have any children?" The point isn't to pry, but to show an interest in the things that matter to the other person. Sometimes an item of clothing (such as a logo on a tee-shirt) or a book the person's reading will provide a good opportunity to break the ice and move the conversation forward: "So you're a Cowboys fan? Did you see that game yesterday?" "Is that a good book? What's it about?"

Next Steps

After breaking the ice, the next steps we should take often become apparent naturally through the flow of the conversation. Sometimes, a person who's going through a significant crisis in their life will open up and begin to talk about it. This happens because they have a sense that we're truly interested in what they're saying and are there to support them. When someone opens up, it's important that we set aside any preconceived agenda we may have for the conversation and switch into listening, affirming, and comforting mode. At other times, there may not be any apparent crisis, but rather just a friendly interchange of pleasantries. In this case, it's generally good to try to naturally transition the conversation to more specifically spiritual matters.

Transitioning to Spiritual Matters

One of the most helpful tools to transition the conversation at this stage is to ask the question, "How important is spirituality or faith to you?" We're aware that the words *spirituality* and *faith* mean different things for different people. Some tie these terms in their mind to a Bible-based Christian faith, while others may practice some other religion, or have a more generic concept of faith and spirituality that's not tied to any one religious tradition. Our choice in using these words is intentional. It gives people an opportunity to express things in their own words without any presuppositions.

By this time, it may already be apparent that the person is a professing Christian. If this is the case, it may be appropriate to change the wording of the question to something like, "How important is your walk with the Lord Jesus to you?" But if, on the other hand, we're still not clear regarding a patient's religious background, beliefs, or practices, it's sometimes helpful to ask a follow-up question: "Do you identify with a religion? If so, which one?" At this point, it's important to respond both verbally and non-verbally in a non-judgmental manner. If they say, for example, that they're Muslim, it's good to follow up with a comment such as, "Tell me a little bit more about your religion and what it means to you." Another good follow-up question is, "What's the one thing you wish all the world knew about your faith?" If they say they're atheist, it's important to maintain acceptance. Many atheists can feel alienated by spiritual conversations. Some possible follow-up comments may be, "Have you always been an atheist or was there some situation or circumstance in your life that led you to move in that direction?"

It's important to show sincere interest in every person's religious perspective. But be careful to not dishonestly give the impression that you agree with things that you don't really agree with. Tact is key. But giving a false impression of agreement will only undermine your credibility to share Christ at a later time.

We should note that in our experience there are times when certain people will say things just to get a reaction from you. Whenever this happens, we should try not to appear overly affected. Don't fight back. Try to keep the line of conversation open.

Follow-Up Questions

At this point, there are a number of different follow-up questions that may be helpful. You'll need to use your common sense, conversation skills, and the guidance of the Holy Spirit regarding how best to proceed. Here are a few options we've found helpful:

- How interested are you in growing in your spirituality or faith? How interested are you in growing or moving beyond where you are?

- What do you do to grow your faith? What are some tips you could give me?

- How often do you get a chance to . . . pray, read the Bible, go to church, etc.? Do you need some support to help you?

- Did you grow up in church? Is there anyone who was an important spiritual role model for you?

- If you once went to church but no longer do, what was it that made you change your mind?

- Do you have anyone in your relationship network who's a positive spiritual influence on you?

- What are some meaningful experiences you've had that have impacted your spirituality or faith?

- Tell me, when I mention the name Jesus, what comes to mind?

- What's your testimony today? Tell me what the Lord's doing in your life.

- Do you mind if I share my testimony?

Whichever of these questions or approaches seems best at the time, it's important to maintain a conversational tone throughout the visit and avoid making the person feel as if they're being interrogated or are the object of a demographic survey. Other than that, I almost always switch into conversation mode. But I'm always listening and making mental notes on the answers to all these questions.

Another set of questions that is often helpful has to do with their faith community or church. One good question to ask is, "Do you have a specific faith community that you consider to be a spiritual home?" Another good question is, "How often do you spend time around others in that community?" Unless I already know or sense that the person isn't traditionally Christian, I usually just ask, "Do you go to church somewhere?"

Just as in the case of someone from a non-Christian religious background, it's important at this point to avoid judging their answer. Our purpose isn't to proselytize for our church or denomination of choice, but to gently guide people forward in their spiritual growth and walk with God. In some cases, we may be familiar with the church or faith community the person mentions. If we have something positive to say about it, it's often good to do so. At other times, it may be the first time we've heard about this particular group—in which case, we should show a genuine interest. Here are a few suggested questions:

- Tell me about that church. How long have you been going there? How did you first hear about that church? What do you like the best about that church?

- How often do you get a chance to attend?

- What are some of the activities your church offers?

It's important to ask these questions in a non-judgmental tone. You want to avoid making the person feel like they're being put on the defensive. At times, people respond, "I believe in God, and I'm a Christian, but I don't go to church," or, "I don't think you need to go to church to be a Christian." Whenever we receive a response like this, it's good to draw the person out and allow them to explain why they feel the way they do. Often, it's due to some situation in the past in which they felt they were emotionally wounded in some way. Whether the person is justified or not for feeling the way they do, we want to help them to reach some spiritual healing. Hopefully, we can help them return to a place in their life where they're open to receiving the ministry of a spiritually healthy faith community. At this point, our willingness to listen and empathize may help them move past the hurts to move forward in their spiritual life once again.

A helpful question for someone who doesn't have a church may be:

- Can I suggest a local church where you can find a faith community to grow?

Or if someone does have a church:

- How much does your faith community influence you to make a positive change in your life?

Another helpful couple of questions are:

- How much does your faith community influence you to make a positive change in your mental health?

- Do you have any special needs in which your faith community is unable to support you?

At times, this last question may lead someone to talk more openly about specific struggles they're dealing with, such as addictions, anxiety, or depression. This may be an appropriate moment to refer them to some resource or ministry that's focused toward helping people with these particular needs. A referral to needed support may be the best ministry we can offer someone in our spiritual conversation.

Another set of questions is directed toward those whom we sense already have a saving relationship with Christ. These questions aim at identifying some area for growth and encouraging them to take that next step in their walk with the Lord. Some possible questions to ask at this stage are:

- What are some spiritual or faith practices you regularly use to grow in your faith?

- What spiritual or faith practice have you not used as much as you would like recently?

At this point, it's good to have some practical tools to help people grow. For example, some people say they don't read the Bible because it's too hard to understand. It can be helpful to lead them to a modern version or a Bible app. We like to have several copies of Bibles available in English, Spanish, Arabic, or other languages that we can give to those who express an interest. It may be helpful to ask, "Can I give you a Bible or devotional to begin a daily Bible reading plan?" If they have a smartphone, we like to point them to the YouVersion app, demonstrate the audio function, and introduce them to modern versions such as the NLT, CEV, or NIV. It may also be helpful to open up the Bible and show them the index and go over some Bible reading basics. There are several good websites to which you can point people to help them get started reading the Bible.

By the same token, some people may need pointers on prayer. In some cases, it may be good to give them a SMART goal, such as spending fifteen minutes each morning in Bible reading, prayer, and journaling.

Here are some other questions you can ask:

- What are some areas in which you would like to grow in your faith?

- How much do you think your faith influences other areas of your life such as family, relationships, work, or community involvement?

- How much do you think your spirituality influences your physical health?

- How much do you think your spirituality influences your mental health?

- How strongly does your faith influence your daily decisions (such as how to use your time or spend your money)?

- How often does your faith motivate you to serve others? What's one example of a time your faith motivated you to serve other people?

- I'm going to list some areas. Stop me if one of these is an area where you feel you could use some coaching or help: finances, relationships, marriage, parenting, job skills, employment, addiction . . .

- Some additional questions that may be especially helpful are the following:

- Are there any beliefs you have a hard time accepting or living out related to your religion?

- What's your biggest spiritual question? What's the biggest faith question that's been holding you back?

We may need to be prepared to present some well-thought-out answers to issues that arise upon asking these last two questions. Some people may indicate, for example, that they have trouble accepting the accuracy of the Bible. Some may have questions about human suffering or what happens to those who've never had a chance to hear the gospel. There are any number of questions or issues that may arise. We won't have and don't have to have the perfect answer for every question. But it's important to communicate empathy with the validity of the question, offer any helpful information we may have that provides some clarity and genuinely seek answers with the person.

Sharing Scripture

It's very helpful to have a passage of Scripture ready to share at some point during the visit. I find this is so important that I prefer not to bog the conversation down with too many questions in order to make sure there will be a bit of time at the end of the visit to present the Scripture passage. I have a handful of favorite passages I like to read and comment briefly on. Some of these passages are better suited for those who I sense have not yet come to a place of faith. Others are better suited for those who already have a personal relationship with the Lord and could just use a bit of encouragement or stimulus to grow in their faith. Personally, I like to read a passage that has between three to six verses in a modern translation that gets the main point across very clearly, and then spend just a few moments explaining the main points of the passage that I feel may be helpful for that person to consider.

A verse we mentioned earlier, Matt 13:52, says, "So [Jesus] told them, 'Every student of the Scriptures who becomes a disciple in the kingdom of heaven is like someone who brings out new and old treasures from the storeroom'" (CEV). I have a handful of passages that I consider to be my treasures that I bring out of the storeroom of my heart and my mind to share at the proper moment. It's good to have the tried-and-true oldies-but-goodies, but also to have new, fresh thoughts from God's Word to share from your personal devotional time whenever the opportunity presents itself. Some of my favorite passages to share on these occasions are Ps 34:4–10 (CEV), Jer 29:11–12 (NLT), Is 30:18–21 (CEV), Is 40:27–31 (CEV), and Hab 3:17–19 (CEV).

Drawing to a Close

At this point in the conversation, it may be time to draw the conversation to a close. Here are some of the things that may be helpful to say at this point:

- Do you have any other thoughts on any of the questions I asked you or any thoughts on something related to these questions?

- Can I pray for you? If so, is there something specific I can pray about for you?

It's important at this point to pray sincerely and to mention their requests specifically. For many people, it may be the first time someone has ever prayed for them personally. Don't underestimate the power of prayer. Let the Holy Spirit guide you as you pray. Don't go on and on, causing them to wonder when you're ever going to end. Do pray with emotion and with power, as the Lord guides you to pray. Pray like you truly believe there is an almighty God who's attentive to your prayer.

Tools for Going Deeper

On other occasions, you may feel that the time is right to draw out the conversation a little more. In our spiritual conversations, it's important to know how to move the conversation to a deeper level as naturally as possible. There are various strategies that can help us to do this. You may want to simply ask, "Can I tell you about my faith in Jesus Christ?" You may ask, "Can I share my testimony?"

The Throne Room

One of my (David) favorite tools when speaking with patients at my clinic at Christ Community Health Services is something I call the Throne Room. The Throne Room is something I use with patients with whom I've been able to establish some degree of rapport and with whom I know I'll have at least five or ten minutes available to continue the conversation before praying for them. Here's what I do. Let's call this patient Bill.

"Bill, I'd like to get you to do something with me. I'd like you to imagine something with me."

Almost always, I get a positive response. Sometimes a patient will close their eyes and say, "Okay, I'm ready."

Then I say, "Okay, Bill, here's what I'd like you to imagine. I'd like you to imagine you had the opportunity to make a one-day visit to heaven."

Then I throw in the following clarification: "Now I'm not talking about dying and going to heaven. I'm just talking about a one-day visit. After you're done, you'll have to come back to earth, okay?"

"Okay."

"All right, imagine you're up there in heaven taking the tour, looking at all the beautiful things, and you come to a door. And on that door there's a sign that says 'Throne Room.' And so you work up your courage, and you go ahead and open the door and look inside, and there in the middle of the room is a throne. And sitting on the throne you see God. And in his hand he's holding a scepter. And as you enter the room, he pulls out the scepter and points it at you and says, 'Bill.' If something like that were to happen, what would your emotional response be? What would you be feeling?"

Now at this time I get many different answers. Some people hesitate a bit. In this case, I try to assure them, "There's no wrong answer. I just want to know what you'd feel."

At this point in the conversation, according to how they respond, I can often get a fairly good idea of their conception of God, and even in some cases I may be able to discern some of the issues that may be a barrier to growth in their relationship with God.

No matter how they respond, though, next I say something like, "You know, I've asked that same question to a lot of people, and I've gotten a lot of different answers. Some people say something like, 'It would be wonderful! I'd feel a great peace come over me!' But you know what some people say? Some people say, 'I'd be scared to death!' And if you think about it, there may be a very good reason to feel that way. You know, you don't just walk into the presence of a king without being invited. Imagine you catch him in a bad mood. It could end up pretty badly for you, couldn't it? It might even be off with your head!"

All the while, I'm paying attention to their non-verbal language. Sometimes at this point they may appear a bit alarmed. At this moment I quickly add, "In this case, though, it's actually good news! First of all, remember this is God, and God doesn't have mood changes. He's not in a good mood one day and a bad mood the next. And besides that, if you know something about ancient history, you know that when a king pulled out the scepter and pointed it at you, that was good news. That was the way he had of saying, 'It's okay. I recognize you. You can come on in. As a matter of fact, come right on up to the throne, and I'd like to talk with you. I'd like you to tell me what I can do for you. Now remember, though, I'm the king, so I've got lots of power. And besides that, I'm not just any king; I'm God. So, I already knew you were coming. And I've been thinking about it. I've been thinking, "I sure would like to do something special for Bill today." So, Bill, what is it you would like me to do for you?'"

Each conversation in which I lead someone on an imaginary journey to the Throne Room is distinct. But on various occasions this moment has proved to be a spiritual breakthrough in my conversation with them. It's at this moment that I've sometimes seen people open up and begin to tell me about their deepest fears or pains. Others tell me about their hopes and dreams. I've even seen people begin to sob. All the while, I'm listening intently and affirming what they say with my non-verbal cues.

Once I feel I've given them the chance to say everything they wanted to say, I say, "Now let me tell you why I wanted to do this exercise in imagination with you today. First of all, if you believe in the spiritual world, you know that it's not imaginary; it's real! There really is a heaven. And there really is an all-wise, all-powerful, and very good God on the throne of heaven. Now, the part about the scepter, I made that part up. But I made it up in order to make a point that's a true point. And that point is that this all-wise, all-powerful, very good God is thinking about you. And not just on certain occasions. It's like every day, 24/7, he sees you there at the door and says, 'Bill!!! So good to see you!! I've been thinking about you! Come on in! Come on in! I've got some special things I'd like to do for you today. But most of all, I'd just like to spend some good one-on-one time with you. Come on in, Bill!'"

Then I say, "I just wanted to help you to understand better about who God is and what he's thinking about you today. And I was thinking that maybe, let's say sometime next week, when you're feeling a bit down and thinking to yourself that no one really understands you or cares what you're going through, you might remember this, and remember that there's a God in heaven who knows exactly what you're going through, and who's there to help you, whatever the case might be. And besides that, I'd like to pray for you. And I've found that this little exercise is a great way for me to learn better just how I can pray for you, because most often, that thing you would ask God to do for you is the exact thing I probably need to be praying about whenever I pray for you. So, are you ready to pray? Let's pray."

Now all this is like a general script for how this conversation might go. But while I'm saying these things, I make a special point to listen to what Bill is saying and to give him the opportunity to add his thoughts or questions along the way. I do my best to make it a genuine conversation and not an impersonal, memorized script. I've seen God use this tool as a means to open people up to that next step in their spiritual growth. It also helps me identify what might be the best way I can help them in their growth, whether I offer that help right there on the spot or save it for another time.

After I've brought someone before the Throne Room, I often have a fairly good idea of where they stand in their relationship with the Lord and their level of receptivity toward making that next step forward in their growth. When I sense that someone has never truly received the gift of salvation and that they're open to hearing more, I often look for the opportunity to take the conversation to the next step, presenting the plan of salvation. I've found that in my spiritual conversations word pictures are especially effective at helping the listener to stay engaged and understand the point I'm seeking to communicate.

Why Should I Let You into Heaven?

In order to transition from the Throne Room to a gospel presentation, I often say something like this: "You know what? I can tell that you're open to learning more about God and how to grow in your relationship with him. I've just asked you to imagine a one-day trip to heaven, and I said I wasn't talking about going to heaven after you die. But I'd like to change the details a bit now. Let's say this time you did die, and you're not already in heaven but are at the gate to heaven, and God meets you there at the gate. And let's say that when he meets you, he says, 'Why should I let you into heaven?' Do you have any idea what you'd say?"

In the Evangelism Explosion training course, they call this a diagnostic question, because it helps you as a gospel witness to diagnose where the person you are talking with stands in their relationship with the Lord. It also gets them to start thinking about their eternal destiny. Generally, someone who already has a personal relationship with the Lord will be able give some sort of an answer that indicates they're not trusting in their own good works or their own good character to save them. Rather, trust in the grace of God extended to us through the forgiveness of sins made possible through the death of Jesus on the cross of Calvary. They may not know how to express it clearly, but the answer someone gives to this question will usually lead you as the evangelist to make some assessment of this person's spiritual condition.

Often someone who doesn't have the assurance of their salvation or who's never truly trusted in Christ will at this point say something like this: "I've lived a good life," or, "I haven't been perfect, but compared to a lot of other people, I've been pretty good."

Others may say, "I don't really know what I'd say. I don't know why he'd let me in."

At this point, I often say something like this: "I'd like to share something with you that can help you know what you could say at that moment and to know that he'd let you into heaven when that moment comes. Would you like to hear it?"

By this time, since I've generally established a certain level of rapport and trust with the person, they'll often say, "Yes, that would be fine."

Tetelestai

It's at this point that I might pick up a box of Kleenex that is available in the patient room and say, "I'd like to use this box of Kleenex as an illustration to help you understand better what I'm getting ready to explain to you. Let's say this box of Kleenex represents your life. And let's say every Kleenex in the box represents some bad deed, word, or even just a bad thought we may have had. In other words, each Kleenex represents what the Bible calls sin. Now the truth of the matter is that each one of us has our own box of Kleenex. And if we're honest about it, each of our boxes is full of a lot of different Kleenex. You've got your box. I've got my box. We've all got our own box."

At this time, I hold the box of Kleenex on top of the open palm of my extended right hand, and I say, "Let's say that God is up in the ceiling and he's looking down, and he sees you, and he wants to have a relationship with you. But there's one big problem. And that problem is that box of Kleenex there on my hand. The problem isn't that God doesn't love us or that he doesn't want to have a relationship with us. The problem is that there's something getting in the way of that relationship he wants to have with us. And that something is our sin."

The Bible says in Isa 59:1–2, "Listen! The Lord's arm is not too weak to save you, nor is his ear too deaf to hear you call. It's your sins that have cut you off from God. Because of your sins, he has turned away and will not listen anymore" (NLT).

"Now when you think about it, this is pretty bad news. If our sins, or the bad things we've done, said, or even thought are getting in the way of our relationship with God and even keeping him from listening to us, that means each and every one of us is in pretty bad shape. We've all got our own box of Kleenex. And it doesn't matter if your box of Kleenex has more Kleenex in it than my box of Kleenex, or if my box has more than yours. When it's all said and done, even if there were just one Kleenex in our box, that would still be enough to provide an impassable obstacle between God and us. The Bible says we've all sinned and come short of God's glory (Rom 3:23) and that even the good things we've done are like filthy rags in God's eyes (Isa 64:6)."

"But there's also good news." At this point, while I keep the box of Kleenex on the upturned palm of my right hand, I hold out the upturned palm of my left hand with nothing on it and say, "Let's say this other hand doesn't represent me or you, but it represents Jesus. And if you notice this hand, there's something very important that's different about it than the other hand. What is that?"

Bill may answer, "It doesn't have a box of Kleenex."

If he doesn't, I help him with the answer. I say, "Jesus doesn't have a box of Kleenex—because Jesus never sinned. On the day when he was baptized, a voice from heaven said, 'This is my beloved Son, and I'm very pleased with him.' Jesus had a perfect relationship with God the Father because he didn't have any sin to get in the way of that relationship."

"Now if you've ever been to church around Easter time, you may have heard a preacher talk about the seven last words of Christ. That's talking about the seven last words that Jesus said when he was on the cross. We don't have time to talk about each of the seven things he said right now, but I'd like for us to think about the last thing he said when he was on the cross. And in Greek, the language of that time, it was just one word, the word *tetelestai*. In English, it's three words, the words, 'It is finished.' Now why do you reckon he said that? You might think he was just acknowledging his life was coming to an end, that he was getting ready to breathe his last breath. But knowing a little bit about the Greek language and the culture of that time helps us to understand better why Jesus said *tetelestai*, 'it is finished.'"

A number of years ago, there were some archaeologists who discovered a stack of ancient documents written in Greek, and as they began to study these documents, they noticed that every one of them had this word *tetelestai* stamped on them. As they began to translate what the documents said, they realized they were all receipts from a debt collector. And the reason they all had *tetelestai* stamped on them was because the debt that was being collected had been paid in full. In this context, the best translation of *tetelestai* was not 'it is finished,' but 'paid in full.' Someone had been coming month after month, paying off little by little a debt they owed, and then they made the final payment and didn't own anything else. The debt collector stamped on their receipt *tetelestai*, paid in full, "you don't owe anything else, you're free to go."

"Now let's get back to Jesus on the cross. When he said *tetelestai*, what was he really saying? From what the Bible tells us, I believe he was saying that there was a debt that was paid in full."

At this point, I turn my right hand over and place the box of Kleenex on top of the upturned palm of my left hand, and I say, "This is what happened when Jesus died on the cross, and I believe that is why the last word he said was *tetelestai*. Now look at my two hands. What's different about my right hand?"

"It doesn't have a box of Kleenex on it. And what's different about my left hand? It now has the box of Kleenex on it."

"What this represents is what Jesus did for us when he died on the cross. The Bible says that the payment for sin is death. That means that everyone who sins—who does, says, or thinks anything that goes against God's law—is destined to die and—it may sound harsh, but I'm going to say it—go to hell. But when Jesus died on the cross, he was taking the guilt of our sin on himself and he was paying the price that we owed to God on our behalf. When he said *tetelestai*, he was saying the price for our sin was paid in full because he paid it for us. Does that make sense to you?"

"Now look at my right hand again. What is there getting in the way of the relationship God wants to have with you or keeping him from listening to you now? Nothing. That's right! Now that barrier that was getting in the way of our relationship with God has been taken away because Jesus paid the price for our sin when he died on the cross, and he took the debt that we owed away from us. Now it has been paid in full, and we don't owe it anymore!"

"Let's go back now to the gate to heaven where God was asking you, 'Why should I let you into my heaven?' If you were to tell him, 'because I've been fairly good,' he would say, 'It doesn't matter. You still have sin that's getting in the way of our relationship. I can't let you in. If you were to say, 'I may not be perfect, but I was just as good as a lot of other people,' he would say, 'All have sinned and fallen short of my glory. Just one sin is enough to condemn you to an eternity in hell.' But what if you were to reach into your back pocket, so to speak, and pull out a certificate of debt that has the word *tetelestai*, paid in full, stamped on it? You might say, 'I know I don't deserve it. What I deserve is to die and spend eternity in hell, because I've disobeyed you and have done many things you commanded me not to do. But Jesus paid the price for my sin when he died on the cross, and my debt has been paid in full.'" Then God would say, 'Indeed, that is the case. Your sins have been forgiven. The price has been paid. The debt has been cancelled. Come in and enjoy for all eternity the wonderful relationship of love, joy, and peace that I've wanted to have with you all along.'"

Money in the Account

Some people understand the message of the gospel, but they have never received the gift of the gospel. Here's a word picture to help this person understand the concept of the gospel as gift.

"When Jesus died on the cross, he paid the price for our salvation. It wasn't something we paid for ourselves. We could never do that. It was a gift he bought for us. But whenever someone gives you a gift, you've got to receive it before it's really yours. What if someone decided they wanted to give a lot of money? They got your bank account information and deposited that money in your bank account. Would the money be yours? Yes, in theory it's yours. But in order to enjoy the benefits of that money, you're going to have to go to the bank or the ATM and make a withdrawal. In the same way, our salvation and the forgiveness of our sins is a done deal. Jesus has already made the deposit in our account. But in order for us to benefit from that deposit, we're going to have to make a withdrawal. According to the Bible, the way we receive the gift that Jesus has given us is by faith. I can offer you a gift and I can reach out to give it to you. But it's not truly yours until you reach out and take it. In the same way, the free gift of salvation is not truly yours until you receive it by faith."

A Brand-New Car

"Let me share one more illustration to make it perfectly clear. Imagine I wanted to do something very special for you. I wanted to buy you a brand-new car. And let's say it was a very nice car, a dream car, one that cost me 50,000 dollars. I call you over and I say, 'Bill, I really like you, and I wanted to do something special for you, so I saved up my money and I bought you a brand-new car. Here's the key. There it is, right there. It's all yours.' And then you look at me and say, 'Wow, that's wonderful! But you shouldn't have done that. That's too much. Here, let me do something to help out.'

And then you reach in your pocket and pull out a quarter and give it to me. How do you think that would make me feel? Not very good, right? It would be like an insult to me. It would make me feel like you didn't truly understand the effort I'd made to get that car for you, wouldn't it? It would make me feel like you didn't really appreciate it.

In the same way, the gift of salvation that Jesus bought for us didn't just cost him 50,000 dollars. It cost him everything! And when we receive his gift, it's important that we don't accept it with the thought that he's done his part and now we have to do ours. The truth is, no matter what we were able to do to help pay for our salvation, it would never be enough, and it would only be like that quarter from our pocket next to what he's done for us. No, instead of trying to do our part to help pay for our salvation, we just need to take that key from his hands, as it were, say thank you, and begin to enjoy the gift he's given us."

Fully Trusting Christ

If I've gotten this far with someone in a spiritual conversation and I sense they're still paying attention, I generally interpret that as a green light for asking them if they're ready at that moment to receive God's free gift of salvation. If they say that they are, I explain that the way we receive God's gift is through faith. Often, if there's still time, I use the illustration of Blondin and the wheelbarrow that we shared earlier in chapter 5 to help them understand better what true faith entails. If I sense they're ready, I say something like, "Jesus is asking you today if you're ready to get into the wheelbarrow of faith that he is pushing across the Niagara Falls of life. Getting into that wheelbarrow means you're admitting that you can't make it to the other side on your own. But it also means that you believe that he is perfectly able to get you safely to the other side and that you're ready to place your whole life in his hands from this point forward. It doesn't mean that you won't ever mess up and fall into sin again and again. But it does mean that when you do, you're in Jesus' hands, and he'll be there to keep you from falling and to help you to live your life in fellowship with him as you both walk together across the Niagara Falls of life. If you're ready to do that right now, I'd be happy to lead you in a prayer to express your desire to accept Jesus' invitation to get into the wheelbarrow. Some people call this moment 'getting saved.' Others call it 'inviting Jesus into your heart.' Others call it 'conversion.' Others call it being 'born again.' In any case, whatever you call it, it is the beginning point of a whole new life. Are you ready to do that?"

If at this point they say yes, then I explain that they can pray in their own words, or if it would be helpful for them, I can pray, and they can repeat what I say—but only if they truly mean the words they're saying. Just saying the words isn't enough. What really matters is what's in your heart.

At this point, I try to be sensitive to what's happening in that person's heart at the time. If I sense they're not ready yet to get into the wheelbarrow, as it were, I may back off a bit. But if on the other hand I sense the Holy Spirit is ushering them to the point of faith in Christ, I offer them some reassurance and encouragement that this may well be the moment. And if it is, I either give them the chance to pray their own prayer, or I guide them with a prayer of my own to help them to express what's in their heart. Either way, I do my best to follow the prompting of the Holy Spirit at this special and sacred time in this person's life.

Let's Review

Though we've described patient interactions in our setting, you can see that the main contours fit what we've proposed in our framework for spiritual conversations.

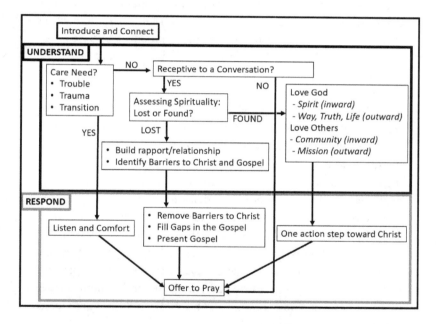

We first begin by listening and understanding. If the person is struggling with something serious, then we just want to show empathy and compassion. We offer to pray, trusting that God is doing his work through our presence rather than our words. If the person doesn't share a serious struggle, we may ask some questions to find out where this person is spiritually and if they're receptive to talking about spiritual things. If they're not receptive, it doesn't do us or them any good to force the conversation. We always want to be sensitive and permission-based. If they seem receptive, then we want to follow up by asking some questions to see if they're a Christian (found) or not (lost). Of course, such hard-and-fast definitions fail, but in our conversations it can help us to know what our next line of questioning might be. If they're lost, we want to learn more about where they are on the Engel Scale and what barriers may be getting in the way of them becoming a Christian. Based on what we learn, we can determine what would be most appropriate and meaningful for this person. If the person is a Christian, then we want to ask questions to identify where they can grow in the four areas we discussed earlier in the chapter. As you ask questions, you can help this person identify one step they can take toward Jesus if they would like to do so. Regardless, at the end of every conversation, we always want to offer to pray with this person. There's great power in prayer.

While in this book we've not handed you a script for having meaningful spiritual conversations, what we've given you is a means of discerning what direction to go. Along the way, we've offered questions to ask, illustrations to use, and even ways of approaching—and perhaps more importantly not approaching—a spiritual conversation. It's our sincere hope that this book will be helpful to you as you seek to honor Christ with any spiritual conversation. And if you've read this far, we trust that is your hope as well. But let's be clear: There's no greater training to help us grow in having spiritual conversations than having them. In the next chapter, we want to challenge you to move past the theory and examples we've presented and to follow through and put these tools into practice as you engage in your own spiritual conversations with others.

9

A Call to Spiritual Conversations

I (JIM) LOVE ANTIQUES Roadshow. I love the drama of seeing people who have no idea what they have come in to find out what their "junk" is worth. Some people really think they have something special, and it turns out to be nothing. Others have something, and they never knew it.

One day I was reading an article about how the most valuable piece on Antiques Roadshow was discovered. A lady had a piece of art hanging on her wall for over forty years and found out that it was worth 500,000 dollars and maybe closer to 1.5 million. Just think about that for a moment! She passed by that painting every day for forty years! She likely had kids wrestling by it, visitors commenting on whether they liked it or not, and maybe even thought about throwing it out in favor of a fresh look. And there were probably many days (even years) when she walked by and didn't take notice at all. Then, one day she looked at it with new eyes and thought, "Hmm . . . I wonder . . . " which led her to the Antiques Roadshow.

Spiritual conversations can be like that. What if we're constantly passing by people of incredible value, but we don't have eyes to see what we are missing? Every day we pass incredibly valuable people in the eyes of God. Sure, they look like normal people to us. They may be grocery store clerks, policewomen, construction workers, even family members and neighbors; but they're God's work of art (Eph 2:10), fearfully and wonderfully made (Ps 139:14) in the image of God (Gen 1:27). But you and I miss incredible opportunities to partner with God in the work that he's doing because we don't stop to see like God sees. A simple, spiritual conversation can be a priceless opportunity to partner with God in the work he's doing in this valuable person's life.

Seeing with Jesus' Eyes

Let me tell you about Grace. When Grace came to Christ Community Health Services, she was lost, prostituting herself to make life work, addicted to drugs, homeless, and had even given her children away because she could no longer care for them. Someone decided to have a simple spiritual conversation with her. That led Grace to begin a relationship with Jesus Christ. Over time, she began to learn about God and his ways and live more of her life for him. She went to rehab, got sober, and eventually pieced her life back together. She got a job, got married, got a home, and even re-established a relationship with her kids. Today, Grace works on our team with our homeless population using the very framework we've sought to teach in this book. And it all started because someone looked at her with Jesus' eyes and thought, "Hmm . . . I wonder . . . " which led to Jesus changing Grace's life.

If we've not been intentionally seeking to have spiritual conversations, we've probably missed the Graces in our life. We pass by people who in the eyes of God have great value, and he wants to use us to help them grow closer to him; but we miss it in all our busyness because we don't have eyes to see.

You probably have a lot on your plate. You might be working a full-time job or even multiple jobs. You might be going to school. You might be raising kids. In the midst of everything, you're trying to pay your bills, run your errands, prepare meals, do chores, and just attend to the many things that life demands. In the midst of it all, you find time to go to church and invest in your own spiritual walk. And I hope you're taking time to rest and relax as well. The activities we have keep us very busy, and they're all probably really good things. We're not saying (necessarily) that you need to get rid of the things you're doing. You want to honor God with the things you do, and that is good. But every day, all along the way, you pass people. Do you really see those people you pass every single day? Friends, strangers, family members, and neighbors; people who are of incredible value to God and are in desperate need of you to have a spiritual conversation that demonstrates God's love and grace to them. Did you miss them?

I (Jim) had seen my next-door neighbors a number of times but hadn't really taken the time to get to know them. They are an older couple who live somewhere else but own a house next to me simply so that they have a place to stay when they visit their grand-children. Knowing they wouldn't be there often, I didn't bother taking the time to invest in that relationship.

One day, I noticed a leak coming from their house. I had their number, so I called to let them know. As we were on the phone, the wife said to me, "I've been battling cancer for a while, and it's not go-ing well at all. I'm not sure I'm going to make it." She was scared. She was likely asking all kinds of questions about life, death, salvation, and God. And I realized that I'd failed to stop and talk to her before now. It took her telling me she thought she was dying of cancer for me to see her as a person God would want me to serve.

In Matt 9:36–38, Jesus encouraged his followers to see people differently. Using the analogy of a harvest to describe how we should see, he said, "When he saw the crowds, he had compas-sion for them, because they were harassed and helpless, like sheep without a shepherd. Then he said to his disciples, 'The harvest is plentiful, but the laborers are few; therefore, pray earnestly to the Lord of the harvest to send out laborers into his harvest.'"

Jesus looked at the crowd of people before him, and his heart filled with compassion. They needed a relationship with Jesus, and he wanted them to experience his love, healing, and grace. So, what's the problem? Jesus says the harvest is ready. What's the harvest? The harvest is what happens when the Word of God is sown in the good soil of a responsive person's heart (Luke 8:15) as they hear it, hold to it, and produce fruit with perseverance. There are many people who are ready to experience a relationship with God and grow in him. So why doesn't it happen? The problem,

Jesus says in Matt 9, is the laborers. The problem is that there are not people who are going out and collecting the harvest. This book was written to equip you for that labor.

Often, we think that people don't want to have spiritual conversations. You know the old saying, you're not supposed to discuss religion or politics with people. That has not been our experience. Over 97 percent of the people we encounter say yes when we ask if we can pray with them. Many of those will share with us where they are spiritually and even listen as we respond in the ways we've described in this book. All of us in our heart of hearts want the love, healing, and grace that only God can provide. That's not the problem; the problem is not that people are turned off to spiritual conversations. The problem is that *we* are not looking at people with the eyes of Jesus. The laborers are not going into the harvest.

Jesus and the Practical Art of Spiritual Conversation

In John 4, Jesus had just finished having what was a life-changing conversation with an adulterous woman who was Samaritan. This was scandalous. Samaritans were hated by Jews and were the most despised nationality at that time. It didn't help that she was certainly not a prime candidate for church membership. In fact, she'd probably never set foot inside of a church if she were alive today. She was considered trash by the Jews and was struggling morally. Most people would have walked on by her and never given her a second thought. But Jesus, while getting some water from the well, saw her. He saw her need and responded.

Picking up the story, the disciples were just returning from getting food in town and were surprised to see him having a conversation with this scandalous woman.

> *Meanwhile the disciples were urging him, saying, "Rabbi, eat." But he said to them, "I have food to eat that you do not know about." the disciples said to one another, "Has anyone brought him something to eat?" Jesus said to them, "My food is to do the will of him who sent me and*

> *to accomplish his work. Do you not say, 'There are yet*
> *four months, then comes the harvest'? Look, I tell you, lift*
> *up your eyes, and see that the fields are white for harvest"*
> (John 4:31–35).

In this passage, Jesus was watching for opportunities to do God's work. After his spiritual conversation with the Samaritan woman, the disciples came back from getting food and walked right past her. They missed her completely. Probably a little annoyed, he said, "lift up your eyes, and see that the fields are white for harvest," basically saying, "Hey, get your head in the game; you just passed a woman who needs my grace and love." The disciples were about to learn a lesson from Jesus about spiritual conversations. He told them that spiritual conversations are about watching, welcoming, and working. If we're wise, we'll listen for ourselves as well.

Watching

The disciples had passed her on the way into town and on the way out of town. The disciples weren't used to looking for those opportunities. In those days, men weren't likely to just walk up and talk to a woman, particularly a woman known to be caught in adultery. It would be sketchy. Not only that, but Jews didn't talk to Samaritans. While the disciples saw an adulterous Samaritan woman who was unworthy of their time, Jesus saw a valuable human being in need of his love. Jesus was watching for a conversation just like that. We should do likewise.

My (Jim) wife's uncle said to me one day, "Oh, you wouldn't believe what I found." He then began to describe his most recent junk store trip, something he calls "going picking." On a regular occasion he'll walk into a thrift store or junk shop, pay a few measly bucks, and walk out with thousands of dollars in art. You see, he owns an art gallery. He's found countless pieces of art that are worth thousands of dollars in common places like second-hand stores. I would go into thrift stores and junk shops all of the time and had never even given it a thought that there might be an opportunity to buy something of value until he started telling me his stories. I had to learn how to watch for opportunities from him.

One day I ran across this painting that I thought looked like it could be worth something. After a little Internet research, I discovered that indeed it was. For twelve dollars, I bought a painting valued at around 1,500 dollars. All it took was for me to watch for opportunities.

Similarly, we must watch for opportunities to share God's love with others. God will place them everywhere we go and all along the way. The value of the opportunity is that it not only blesses the person with whom we have the conversation, but it blesses us as well. We see God work through us as we share his love with others.

Watching is an act that involves our heart and mind. It means we follow God's lead and sense what the Spirit is saying to us. It also means we watch to see the people all around us. We listen and understand people on their own terms, trying to see if this person is receptive to a conversation. We watch with the eyes of Jesus, and by his Spirit he'll teach us how to see as he sees. That may mean we need to reexamine our preconceived ideas about whom we interact with, which parts of town we go to, and what the goal of a spiritual conversation is.

The disciples missed the Samaritan woman because in their mind someone "like her" was disqualified and not valuable. Had they been able to see like Jesus sees, they wouldn't have seen an adulterous Samaritan woman. Instead, they would have seen someone who needed Jesus. How many times have we missed an opportunity to share the love of God with someone because we weren't watching? How many times have we passed by someone in need on our way to something we deemed important?

Is there someone in your life that you pass who needs to hear the gospel? Is there a person whom you know needs the love of Christ in their life? Are you watching for the opportunity? Take the time to stop and share. Like Jesus, show interest in the life of the people you pass every day. Tell them about Jesus' love for them.

Welcoming

In the passage from John 4, Jesus welcomed this woman, while most would have disregarded her. He initiated the conversation with her, saying, "Will you give me a drink?" She was even surprised that Jesus welcomed a chance to talk to her. She replied, "You're a Jew, and I'm a Samaritan woman. How can you ask me for a drink?" basically saying, "Why are you talking to me?"

Jesus had a very distinct way of welcoming people. Jesus didn't present himself as powerful or having it all together in the first greeting. No, it was an act of humility to ask her for a drink. Jesus reached out to her, demonstrating that he wasn't too good to speak with her. Jesus asked to drink water served by hands that society had considered too sinful. This simple act of humility was a welcome mat.

When we're going about our lives, whether that is going to church, school, work, or to see family, we must put out our own welcome mats. We do that by being humble and showing more interest in others than in ourselves. We ask them questions and show we genuinely care about them. At times, this will make us uncomfortable. But we must offer a welcome to people.

Welcoming people involves two things: our inward attitude and our outward attitude. Jesus' inward attitude was one that welcomed any opportunity to serve. He felt nourished by the goodness of doing God's work. It was not a burden to him to stop and talk with someone. He wasn't afraid of connecting with someone even if that "someone" was scandalous. He feasted on doing God's will. Even when people shunned or rejected him, he welcomed the opportunity to do God's will and connect with others.

Outwardly, his attitude was that of grace and love. Jesus reached out to this outcast woman. It was this act of welcoming that caused her to accept his message. The outward attitude of welcoming is not about judging people, nor predetermining their response, but welcoming the opportunity, even with people we think we shouldn't welcome.

In his book *End of the Spear*, Steve Saint tells the story of an unlikely friend. In 1956, Steve was five years old when his father, Nate, flew an airplane with four other missionaries into the jungles of Ecuador and dared to make contact with the most dangerous tribe known to man, the Waodani. After several months of exchanging gifts in order to build trust with the natives, the five missionaries were speared multiple times and hacked to death with machetes.

One of the men in the tribe was Mincaye. Years later, Steve found out that Mincaye was the one who delivered the final spear that ultimately killed his father. Today, Steve Saint and Mincaye, who killed Steve's father, consider themselves family and harbor no resentment toward each other. Mincaye became a Christian because Steve's dad, and ultimately Steve, welcomed the opportunity to share with him. Steve's dad paved the way to his salvation by welcoming the chance to share, even if it meant death.

Steve says he has never forgotten the pain and heartache of losing his dad. It would have been understandable for Steve to consider Mincaye unworthy. Steve said, "I can't imagine not loving Mincaye, a man who has adopted me as his own, and the other Waodani." Steve welcomed the opportunity to love God by loving Mincaye, a person he probably felt like he shouldn't welcome. And Mincaye is now not only a Christian, but because of Steve's radical love, a surrogate father to him.

The mission field you are called to may not be in distant lands like Ecuador, but there are opportunities for significant spiritual conversations all around you. We need to have our eyes open to watch, but we also need to welcome people and show the same type of love that Jesus showed. We welcome these opportunities by being willing and ready in our hearts to serve God, even in uncomfortable ways or in uncomfortable places with people who make us uncomfortable. Often, we'll find that we'll be more blessed for taking the opportunity, just like Steve was blessed for loving Mincaye.

Working

In John 4:34, Jesus tells us his food is to do the work of the one who sent him. Jesus tells us very clearly that the harvest is ready. Jesus tells his disciples in verse 38 to open their eyes and see that the fields are white unto harvest: "I sent you to reap that for which you did not labor. Others have labored, and you have entered into their labor." As we mentioned earlier, in Matt 9:37 we are told that the harvest is plentiful, but the laborers are few. Jesus didn't consider people's receptivity to the gospel to be the problem. Instead, he considered the problem to be the lack of work on behalf of his people.

In the passage with the Samaritan woman, Jesus talked about the labor. He said that the harvest is ready, if we just go out and get it. He goes so far as to tell his disciples that they'd be reaping that for which they'd not labored. Reaping the harvest is easy, but it actually involves going out and doing the work.

Imagine a farm. On this farm there are several fields with crops of every kind. There's a large family living in the farmhouse, as well as the farmer. When that time of year comes around, the farmer announces to his children: "The harvest is ready!" What if, when the harvest is ready, the children stay indoors to work instead of going out to the fields to work? Some of the children clean the toilets, some start doing laundry, while others are sweeping and vacuuming. Some of the farmer's children even sit back and enjoy the benefits of the work but do nothing at all.

What will happen to the crops? While the house is clean, everyone is going to starve because the harvest will never be gathered. Working in the house is important and needs to be done. But the most important work is outside. If the harvest is ready, it's time to get to work.

Don't we do that sometimes? We love our churches. We love getting to be in community with others, singing worship songs, learning from God's Word, and maybe even serving in significant ways. And that needs to be done, no question. But, sometimes, we're so busy doing stuff inside the church that we forget to get out and work in the fields. Do you ever get so busy in God's house that you forget the work outside? Many of us are so busy with other things that we never reach out to the people all along the way who desperately need to hear about the love, healing, and grace found in a relationship with Jesus.

We're not suggesting that church is bad, work is bad, school is bad, or home is bad. We're not suggesting that we have to be out spending our every waking moment in spiritual conversations with others. That would be taking it to the opposite extreme. But are you out talking to *anyone*? Are you doing *anything* to share God's Word with people? Can you think of one conversation you've had with someone about Jesus in the last month?

Are You Ready?

It's our earnest prayer that this book will be a help to you. We hope that you feel more equipped in the practical art of spiritual conversation so that you can meaningfully and substantially encourage each person to take that one step further toward Christ. We hope that you see that this is not just about *evangelism* nor is it just about *discipleship*. This is about helping any willing person move closer to Christ, regardless of whether they're a staunch atheist or a seasoned believer.

It's our prayer that the once eager evangelist now knows when it may be inappropriate or even harmful to share this good news. We trust that this person is more equipped to have meaningful conversations with not just the lost but also with the hurting and the found. It's our prayer that the many who love Jesus and walk with him but never seem to get around to having spiritual conversations with anyone know how they can lovingly and thoughtfully engage a person spiritually, share the gospel more, and help others progress in their love for Jesus.

It's our prayer that the many who feel stuck in their discipleship efforts may have a bigger vision of what it means to have a relationship with Christ. We pray you are more equipped to help fellow sojourners when they also feel stuck. It's our prayer that those who before could see no connection between the gospel as they have received it and the many important things they do each day now know that God cares deeply about even seemingly mundane activities and that they can truly integrate their faith into everything they do.

The general framework is simple enough. In our spiritual conversations we need to first seek to *understand* and then *respond*. God has done his part. He's prepared the harvest. The harvest is ready. Are you?

Bibliography

Aldrich, Joe. *Lifestyle Evangelism*. Colorado Springs: Multnomah, 1981.

Barrs, Jerram. "Francis Schaeffer: The Man and His Message." *Reformation 21* (2006). https://www.covenantseminary.edu/francis-schaeffer-the-man-and -his-message/

Beauchamp, Tom L., and James F. Childress. *Principles of Biomedical Ethics*. 5th ed. Oxford: Oxford University Press, 2001.

Carnegie, Dale. *How to Win Friends and Influence People*. New York: Simon and Schuster, 1936.

Doran, Miller, et al. "There's a S.M.A.R.T. Way to Write Management's Goals and Objectives," *Management Review* 70 (1981) 35–36.

Engel, James F., and Wilbert Norton. *What's Gone Wrong with the Harvest?* Grand Rapids: Acadamie, 1975.

Green, Keith. "What's Wrong with the Gospel? Section 2: 'The Added Parts.'" https://lastdaysministries.org/Articles/1000008643/Last_Days_Ministries /LDM/Discipleship_Teachings/Keith_Green/Whats_Wrong_With. aspx?page=1

Hofstede, Geert. "National Cultures in Four Dimensions: A Research-Based Theory of Cultural Differences among Nations." *International Studies of Management & Organization* 13 (1983) 46–74.

Plantinga, Cornelius, Jr. *Not the Way It's Supposed to Be*. Grand Rapids: Eerdmans, 1996.

Saint, Steve. *End of the Spear*. SaltRiver: Carol Stream, 2005.

Scroggins, Jimmy, and Steve Wright. *Turning Everyday Conversations into Gospel Conversations*. Nashville: B&H, 2016.

Singlehurst, Laurence. *Sowing, Reaping, Keeping*. 2nd ed. London: IVP UK, 2006.

Steer, Roger. *Hudson Taylor: Lessons in Discipleship*. Philadelphia: OMF International, 1995.

The Neighborhood Christian Clinic. "Spiritual Care Curriculum." https://www. thechristianclinic.org/spiritual-care-curriculum/

Warren, Rick. *The Purpose Driven* Life. Exp. ed. Grand Rapids: Zondervan, 2012.

Willard, Dallas. *The Great Omission.* San Francisco: Harper, 2006.

Willard, Dallas, and Keith Giles. "The Gospel of the Kingdom." (2005). http:// old.dwillard.org/articles/artview.asp?artID=150

CPSIA information can be obtained
at www.ICGtesting.com
Printed in the USA
JSHW040218220521
15005JS00004B/12

9 781725 294813